THE WOMAN RUNNER

Free to Be the Complete Athlete

GLORIA AVERBUCH

Cornerstone Library
Published by Simon & Schuster, Inc.
New York

Since women's running is making history moment by moment,
the information in this book is current as of April 1984.
Any new information will be recorded in later editions.

Produced by The Miller Press, Incorporated
Copyright © 1984 by Gloria Averbuch and The Miller Press, Inc
Original photographs Copyrighted© 1984 by Ken Levinson
All rights reserved
including the right of reproduction
in whole or in part in any form
Published by Cornerstone Library
A Division of Simon & Schuster, Inc
Simon & Schuster Building
Rockefeller Center
1230 Avenue of the Americas
New York, New York 10020

CORNERSTONE LIBRARY and colophon are registered trademarks
of Simon & Schuster, Inc.

10 9 8 7 6 5 4 3 2 1
Manufactured in the United States of America

Library of Congress Cataloging in Publication Data
Averbuch, Gloria (date)
     The woman runner.

     Bibliography: p.
     Includes index.
     1. Sports for women.   2. Running.   1. Title
GV709.A94 1984   796'.01'94   84-9528
ISBN: 0-346-12644-4

Book design: H. Roberts Design

Dedication

To Sandra Keaton (December 12, 1952–February 7, 1980),
who fought so bravely
and helps me to remember the privilege of being alive

Acknowledgments

Thanks to my father, Bernard Averbuch, who taught me I can; my mother, Frances Slater, for her intelligence; my husband, Paul Friedman, for creative input and holding life together day to day; Holly Halse, for over twenty years of friendship; Angela Miller, for her enthusiasm and support.

The New York Runners Club for its continuous support; The Avon International Running Circuit for use of its excellent research files and photos, and for the help of its staff; Mimi Fahenstock for the Resource List and history research; Dan Schlesinger for his articulate account of Japanese women's running; Toni Reavis for his notes on Joan Benoit; Isabelle Carmichael for being the "cover girl" for the book.

Contents

Introduction

AN estimated seventeen million women in the United States run, and millions more around the world are joining them. Only a little over a decade ago not one woman completed the New York City Marathon. Today it is the largest women's marathon field in the world, with over twenty-eight hundred entrants. In 1979, *The New York Times* honored Grete Waitz for her world marathon record with an editorial that asked when women distance runners would have their day in the Olympics. That day has come with the inclusion of the first women's Olympic marathon in 1984, and so has the women's running boom.

One need only turn on television, open a magazine, or walk through any park in any city to witness the astounding effect of women's running. Major media have highlighted the new women's athletic beauty, and physical fitness permeates our entire society. In short, it's in to be fit, to be an athlete, to project beauty and strength in a new way.

What does a world of women aspiring to fitness tell us? How did it come to be? How does society reflect the change in women? How do women who want to run or compete get started? What should every woman runner know? This book answers these questions.

The Woman Runner is much more than a running book. It celebrates a new wave of athleticism. It examines the philosophical aspects of how the woman runner views the world, and how she is changing it. Based on a survey of close to a thousand women runners (see Appendices), the book deals with the topics of greatest interest. The survey also reveals how important it is for women to read about what's going on within and around themselves, a major theme in *The Woman Runner*.

Sports used to be a man's world, but now it is for all of us to share.

Times are changing and women's running is changing with them. Over six thousand women at a time have run in all-women's races in cities in every part of the United States and in countries from Brazil to Ireland.

Testimony of women everywhere reveals that we are bound today by a new camaraderie. Together we are realizing our physical abilities and discovering the joy of doing for ourselves, because not money, man, or machine can give a woman what she gives herself when with her own initiative and strength she takes her first running steps, or crosses the finish line.

I wrote this book from the vivid memories and experience of a lifelong involvement in competitive athletics, as a runner for the past ten years, as a staff member of the New York Road Runners Club, and from a strong belief in the personal and social value of sports

We are millions of women who have rediscovered our athletic selves. This is a book for us, and for those who share our lives and our goals. We know that women's running has arrived, and we are proud to be women athletes.

Gloria Averbuch

Part I
The Woman Athlete

My 25th Birthday

Today
I came out of the starting blocks for the first time.
pushed back on the legs I had trained so well,
stretched my calf muscles and kicked out the kinks
before tenderly placing my feet in the blocks.

My hands,
arched over a line on the textured rubber surface of the track,
quivered with the weight of my body.
"You are unprepared," they told me,
and I knew, in this sliver of time that had become my whole life,
how much I could respect that voice.

Runners set . . .
the muscles, so totally belonging to one another,
knew just what to do.
My body, an accent mark,
spare and strong,
poised in the light track shoes.
a spiked weapon
alert for the battle I have sworn to wage
against all I have not yet done.

The gun.
uncoiling to the reflex of an inner ear,
like a shell that memorizes the sound of an entire sea.
a literal instant
but complete.
an art so unconsidered.

I move out, a coiled body set free.
running towards, not away.
possessed by the athlete's joy of single-mindedness.

A birthday
a new vision, a country I have not seen.
new voices in new tongues,
crying, cheering.
a gift.
an understanding of those who race so well,
of those who know the exquisite power
of total involvement
with fractions of a second.

4/29/76

1

We've Come a Long Way.
Or Have We?

Feminism and Other Influences
on the Running Movement

"**Y**OU'VE COME A LONG WAY," the saying goes about women's progress toward equality, but to what exactly, and from where? Have we reached the end, and if not, how much further is there to go?

The recent growth of women's participation in sports, and the present status of women's running, can be traced to the psychological and social battles women have been waging for at least twenty years. The climate that is conducive to millions of women running in the eighties is a direct result of developments which began back in the sixties.

Growing up in the fifties and sixties, I remember the clear implication of what it meant to be a female athlete: like dance and piano lessons, it was helpful for a girl's general growth, but a phase—something to be passed through, like braces or puberty. Most hobbies or interests were ancillary, because if the only guarantees in life are death and taxes, for a woman it was believed there was a third: marriage.

Today this view of life seems archaic. There is a new celebration of women's athleticism that has never before taken place. Millions of women of all ages are participating in sports; girls are being offered athletic scholarships to college, and there is prize money in road races. And socially speaking, for a woman to beat the guy next to her in a race is no longer something to avoid for fear she'll bruise his ego or won't get a date with him. Not only is she quite unconcerned what effect beating him will have, he'll likely admire her for being able to outrun him.

At first glance, it would seem that feminism and the women's liberation movement are the main force behind the growth in women's running. The movement's principle of equality between the sexes has enabled a woman to take up athletics like her male counterpart. But a closer look reveals that a phenomenon as large as the women's running movement is by nature complex, and therefore has been influenced by many social factors.

In the early sixties one of the main themes of the Kennedy presidency was physical fitness. Studies revealed that Americans were horribly out of shape, with some of the highest disease rates in the world caused by sedentary living. A national 50-mile walk campaign was launched, and the President's fitness council exercises became the basis of physical education class. In my junior high school even the girls achieved a new measure of status for doing the most sit-ups or clocking the fastest quarter mile.

In the late sixties, the rebellion against conformity, specifically the institution of marriage, was a sign that some of the conventions which had kept women one-dimensional were now becoming unpopular. Free of the singular definition of being a wife and given other measures of self-worth, women sensed their world opening up.

However, it was only inadvertently that women found themselves with these expanded choices. Ironically, the initial rebellion against conventions like marriage had very little to do with freeing women specifically, and more to do with disrupting the social order. It was only later that women would take up their own cause in the form of the women's liberation movement.

As a consequence of social rebellion, people became increasingly introspective. Liberation was the spirit of the era, and together with introspection, it encouraged women to assess their roles and images. They took a look at the typical woman's world, and didn't like what they saw.

A new trend in thought and action would irrevocably change society. A woman felt she ought to do more for herself, that she ought to feel better about herself—both in spirit and in body. With marriage and children no longer her singular all-consuming goal, she began to examine herself from within.

A strong surge of individualism accompanied the quest for self-fulfillment. The hippy period of the early sixties was a time for people to do what they wanted, when they wanted, and for their own edification and pleasure. As the youth of this new era, we were raised to believe that we were separate, special; this was the meaning of hippy non-conformity. We were encouraged to harbor the Walter Mitty fantasy of being everyone and doing it all.

It was a sign of the times that many of us in fact believed we could have it all. This translated to athletics as well. No one ever said to me, "You can't play because you're a girl" or "You'll never be any good." Just as one could harbor dreams of becoming President (or in this era, of overthrowing him), so too could one dream of winning an Olympic gold medal.

In protest against the puritan ethic and a mechanized society, a new interest was spawned in body awareness. "Getting in touch with yourself" meant doing so physically as well as emotionally. A greater physical consciousness led to a greater physical freedom, especially for women, many of whom had been raised to be more inhibited. Clothing got lighter and lesser, and the trend was to be less self-conscious. This alleviation of embarrassment over the body in the sixties may have led to the free use of the body for sports in the eighties.

These influences spilled over into the seventies, in which one of the main themes was self-sufficiency. Particularly distressed over the dependence that was symbolized by the Arab oil boycott, the tone in this country was that Americans must never need to rely on anyone again. They wanted to make sure they could do it themselves, individually and as a nation. Distance running became the perfect expression of this principle. Completing a marathon meant making it very far, on very little, by one's own resources: the epitome of self-sufficiency.

Joining physical fitness, the rebellion against marriage, introspection, individualism, and body consciousness came feminism, the final imprimatur and the last and most influential social movement that would allow women their new status in sports.

But before women could develop their athleticism, women's sports had to become accepted by society as a whole. Running wasn't going to be a mass movement for women if they had to take abuse every time they stepped out the door for a run. Something had to make it all right to run through the streets of a big city in clothes that once were worn only in the privacy of one's own home.

When I began running regularly in the early seventies, going for a run was like surviving a war. Even in the most progressive parts of the country I was hooted at, mocked, and mimicked. I was even spit at, chased by drunks, and had a bottle thrown my way. On a visit to New York City in 1974, I armed myself against a barrage of verbal assaults every time I ran the five blocks to Central Park.

It was in 1972 that the cause of women's rights and running joined forces. Twelve women staged a sit-down strike on the starting line of the New York City Marathon, protesting a ruling by the Amateur Athletic Union (AAU) forcing them to start ten minutes before the men's race began. They got up after the ten minutes had passed and ran with the men. Soon thereafter the ruling was changed to allow women to compete equally with men in distance races. This act of open defiance was given support in the general climate of women's protests.

By the time I ran again in New York in 1979, it was as if a revolution had taken place and women runners had emerged victorious. Antagonism has by no means been eradicated today, but it is far from what it was. I can now usually run the five blocks to Central Park without so much as a hoot. Sometimes I even believe we are beginning to be admired when I hear comments like "Looking good" or "Keep up the pace."

Leading feminist Letty Cottin Pogrebin, a writer and an editor at *Ms.* magazine, points out that the first step toward accepting women's sports was that they became "feminized." Women began to wear "cute sport outfits," and modeled sporty clothes. Unfortunately a necessary step in social development, this ultimately allowed women's athletics to become accepted by society. "Ten years ago if a woman had a muscle in her arm she rolled down her sleeve," says Pogrebin. Today, she flexes it.

But most women's sports authorities are quick to point out that only certain sports have achieved acceptance. Most of them are the more feminine and less directly competitive activities. A woman gymnast can be the star of television sports, for example, but that's not likely to happen for a woman shot-putter.

With the increase in the number of women athletes, it becomes more acceptable for others to begin. As Pogrebin points out, "You're not accused of being a jock, a lesbian, or a toughy anymore if you participate in sports." When feminism helped redefine femininity, that definition also included women athletes. Femininity was no longer synonymous with frailty as it had once been. It now included more of the elements of androgyny, an integrated combination of female and male characteristics. So a woman could achieve the balance of being athletic and competitive, and still be considered feminine at the same time.

But Paula Cabot, director of research and education projects for the Women's Sports Foundation in San Francisco, says that for various reasons the women's movement at first ignored women's sports in the sixties, and she claims studies back up her allegation. In those years, she contends, people didn't understand sports for women. In addition, the sixties era was "down on competition," which is of course the basis for most sports. A number of women's sports authorities agree with Cabot that feminists did not include women's sports in the early days of their cause. (Talamini and Page, Elkins, and Boutilier and San Giovanni are some of them.)

Cabot believes that the revolution in women's athletics was caused not by one factor, but by a combination, most of which were social and economic. One of these factors was that women were forced out of the home and into the job market, part of a social shakeup that signaled the redefinition of their roles. Cabot believes that the attack on the educational system illustrated by Title IX was another influence. In addition, the Amateur Sports Act of 1978, which restructured amateur athletics in this country, brought wide attention to sports such as running.

Most women's sports authorities agree that the passage of Title IX was one of the main events that contributed to public awareness of women's sports. A provision of the Higher Education Act of 1972, Title IX outlaws discrimination on the basis of sex in any educational program receiving federal funds. After the passage of the act, it immediately became clear that the greatest discrimination was in the area of women's sports.

The women's movement eventually did contribute to women's sports, claims Paula Cabot. The ideas of being strong, evaluating one's concept of the body, and becoming healthy for oneself as opposed to concentrating on men's needs are among the feminist principles that aided women's sports. These aspects only contributed significantly, however, ten years after the women's movement had caught on, and when women gained a better understanding of sports.

We've come a long way.

In 1979, *The New York Times* editorialized the world record of Grete Waitz in the New York City Marathon. The title of the editorial, "2:27:33—and Waiting," referred to the day when women would run the marathon in the Olympic Games. That day is August 5, 1984.

In 1970 not a single woman completed the New York City Marathon, and there weren't many women even taking a block-long jog. Today more than twenty-eight hundred women, over eighty of whom have run a marathon under the Olympic-qualifying standard of 2:51:16, run through their own finish line in the New York City Marathon.

The women's world records for distance running continue to fall at a rate that leads some experts to believe there may be no limit to how fast women can run in the future. In the brief two years since Alberto Salazar cut a mere 21 seconds off the twelve-year-old men's world marathon record, the women's record has been broken twice and tied once. The new record is a full 2 minutes 46 seconds faster than it was in 1981.

So close, yet so far away.

When American 100-mile record-holder Donna Hudson received a trophy for a race she won, she immediately noticed something was wrong. Surveying the figure of the runner, she slid her thumb across the chest.

Turning to the race organizer, she asked angrily, "Where are the bumps?" Donna, who can run distances most people are reluctant to drive, had been given a man's trophy instead of a woman's.

"Make no mistake," cautions 1984 women's Olympic coach Brooks Johnson, "there's no full-blown revolution in women's running. The door is cracked and a few have escaped, but it's only a crack." Johnson points out that when the number of women in races equals the number of men, we will have achieved parity. Progress will begin only when women outnumber men as they do in the general population. We may have the Olympic marathon for women, but the 5,000 and 10,000 meters are still missing. "Sexism isn't gone," says Johnson, "it's just been redirected."

Men runners, as well as most men athletes, still make substantially more money than women. A list of track and field athletes and the prices they command for track meets in a November, 1983, issue of *Track and Field News* places Carl Lewis as number one with $15,000 per meet; his female counterpart, Mary Decker, is the first woman mentioned, twenty names later. Her price: $1,125 per meet. The arguments are endless: women do the same training; they run the same distance; they provide the same excitement—even a recent survey of the American public shows that 92 percent say men and women athletes should be paid equally. So why the discrepancy in cash?

Following the first World Championships in Helsinki in August 1983, over fifty top women runners from twenty countries filed a sex-discrimination suit in an attempt to force sports authorities to include the 5,000- and 10,000-meter races for women in the 1984 Olympic Games. Two of the women were World Championship gold medalists Grete Waitz and Mary Decker. Why are these events left out of the Olympics? Why should any running event for women be left out? Why do women still make up less than 20 percent of all participants in the Olympic Games?*

Isn't it enough to justify the inclusion of all running events when one considers that the marathon time of world-record holder Joan Benoit (2:22:43) would have won the Olympic gold medal in every *men's* Olympic marathon up to and including 1960?

What will it take? Haven't women gone beyond proving the worthiness of full equality in sports? If times are changing, shouldn't attitudes change as well as minutes and seconds on the track and the roads?

We have in fact come a long way, but it is time to stop coming, or going, anymore. Let's just get there. Let's just be able to say: we've arrived!

---

*Dorothy V. Harris, "Female Sport Today: Psychological Considerations," *International Journal of Sports Psychology,* vol. 10, 1979, p. 170.

2

Rediscovering
Your Athletic Self

We could never have loved the earth so well if we had had no childhood in it . . . What novelty is worth that sweet monotony where everything is known, and loved because it is known.

George Eliot, Middlemarch

MOST OF US once had something we lost, and we grew so far from it that barely a memory remained. No instinct urged us to hunt for it. But a new era has dawned, and with it a new consciousness. We now find ourselves living amidst a collective search, and our entire society has undertaken the quest.

What we have lost is the sense of our physical selves and our physical resources, the ability to use our bodies as instruments of well-being—to help give us strength, happiness, and a sense of being grounded in the world.

Sport is life—a great part of it at least. We tend to forget that training the body to become a fine-tuned machine is equally as important as honing the intellect. The Greeks knew it; the Greek men anyway, who made sport an integral part of their existence. The playing fields and competition were a measure of strength and status, the weave of their social fabric. In sport the Greeks found wholeness.

Today we celebrate the age of athletics for women. By virtue of our numbers and our achievements in the world of sports, we announce that we have truly arrived. We call out to be counted, to be reckoned with, to be respected. Women have found a new arena, and in it we are prospering. We rejoice in our new relationship to each other and to those around us, and we invite the company of those who have not yet joined us.

Our self-discovery begins at birth. All children, girls as well as boys, possess an inherent sense of the adventure to learn. Its first signs are physical. Even the earliest evidence of new life is expressed physically by the movement and kicking in the mother's womb. Babies grab for objects—their way of reaching for the world—and chew on the objects in order to "digest" or understand them. Being physical is a primal instinct, one of our most basic needs, and it is the vehicle for our earliest experiences in facing challenge. We are born with the urge, physical in nature, to seek and understand, and it grows with each new discovery.

Women have an advantage to aid them in realizing the importance of being physical. A woman's connection to the earth and to her physical self has always defined her. It is expressed by childbirth and the initial education (or sometimes lack of it) of women about their bodies. Concepts such as "earth mother" and "mother nature" are not just coincidentally in the feminine gender.

In the sense that women are required to understand their physical selves early in life, biology is in fact destiny. A woman is aware of her body because she is taught to be attuned to it, from the time she plays with baby dolls, to the time she has babies of her own.

It would seem completely logical, then, that so primal a need as integrating the physical self into the personality, something so ingrained in the psyche, would require development throughout life and be as essential as any other nourishment for growth. But somehow, at some time, for what was believed to be progress or perhaps higher status, most of us lost touch with this primal sense, and it was buried or left to atrophy from lack of use.

Like Dorothy in *The Wizard of Oz*, we walk our own yellow brick road looking for the way, for the answer, for that sense of what we have lost, because so instinctively precious is it that we know, more accurately we feel, that something is missing and we must recover it.

Dorothy must undergo trials and conquer fears in order to realize that to find her way she need only look within herself. Yet she must venture forth to discover this—an active explorer, learning to survive. Like Dorothy, we must learn to regain our initial, physical relationship to the world, and when we do we find great joy in discovering our physical capabilities.

These physical capabilities find expression through sport, in which we learn to struggle and survive. We learn about our limits, and surprise ourselves when we manage to surpass them—realizing that self-discovery is endless. Through sport we learn courage, appreciation, commitment, and camaraderie, and when we use our bodies we are back to basics: we feel the privilege of being lively, of being alive.

If these associations seem remote, watch children, and remember your own childhood. Play is their life and their joy, and "child's play" means more than the phrase has come to imply. Every move and every game is part of the socialization process: children learning their physical relation to a physical world, and their relationship to each other. A child must fall many times before walking, reach out many times before being able to catch a ball—just as an adult must stumble and fall throughout life, and lose "the game" to understand winning. Both in childhood and as adults, these are our most basic discoveries.

We never outgrow the need to play. The game may be make-believe, but our need to play it is not. Playing is the act of living out emotions and fantasies in a world of our own making, a world in which everything makes sense because we make the rules. We decide what the stakes are, and can therefore set about controlling, coping with, and "winning" the game.

Our sport, or race, is only the child's play in adult form. If we feel we have outgrown the need to play, it is only because we have forgotten what it provides. We need it to keep growing. Without play we are robbed—like children who are forced to grow up without being taught to grow wise.

If men lost the need to be physical in the twentieth century, working at a desk instead of in a field, and ceased to engage in the sports they once played, women's loss took place even earlier and has been even greater. Long ago active women were relegated to physical inactivity and in addition to basic physical loss, they have traditionally been denied the framework of team sports, and thus have never learned what competitive play has to offer. Most women have never been given the chance to understand what it means to "connect" with the ball—to hear the sweet sound of the pitch hitting the bat—or to catch the perfect pass, run the perfect race, and throughout it all feel not only their own strength and success, but the adulation of peers and onlookers. They have not been able to be the star of the show, a feeling of joy so tangible it makes the blood quicken.

It is these games and the emotions associated with them that often help alleviate some of the discomforts of puberty. Not only do sports help young people temporarily escape from the trials of adapting to a changing world, they also aid in that adaptation by allowing adolescents to experience feelings and learn skills which are useful in later life. In that time of youth when nothing seems to fit, when the requirements of adult life inflict difficult growing pains, adolescents can possibly find relief in what they know: sports. They engage in games which provide challenge and success and which duplicate life—its pitfalls as well as its triumphs.

Books have been written about it, thousands of fiction and nonfiction accounts of boys and their dreams, or the achievements of great athletes who begin their careers in playgrounds and grow to become the stars who make basketballs swoosh through nets or footballs soar across stadiums before thousands of adoring fans. Everyone needs and wants a dream. Girls should be able to be dream-believers too, to find models that show that women can aspire and participate in sports, and that they can experience the success their brothers do.

Sports teach us that losing has a rightful place in our lives, too. One can always read the accounts of both great and lesser athletes who have struggled but lost, yet come back with a new determination to continue the contest. These examples teach us what we must learn not just about sports, but about all of life: that it is not only having made it to the top that counts, but the process of getting there as well.

My earliest memories are of games and sports. I saw everything in life as physical, and everything a part of being physical made me happy: the bats and balls; the smell of leather baseball gloves when first oiled; the fine, dry dirt around the diamond; the changing shapes of the balls throughout the seasons: footballs, basketballs, tennis balls. Each season was defined by a different pair of sneakers, every athlete's symbol of pride. My body told time like a clock, and I relied on it to keep my life in order.

I was a tomboy, and I have been one for most of the over three decades of my life. Admittedly, perhaps sports made more sense to me because I grew up with my father and my brother after my parents divorced. My father practiced sports with us in the evenings, and capitalizing on my ability, I tried hard to excel. I sensed these games were the way of life. My mother's love of dance also conveyed the special meaning of physical endeavors. When I was still very young she enrolled me in ballet class and later I took ice-skating lessons.

I remember competition as being both the most exhilarating and the most painful experience of my childhood. In individual loss, or in the disappointment of the team, I was devastated by hurt and humiliation. I can still see the blur of the streets as my tears accompanied me home from a losing effort.

But winning! Winning brought all the joy I would soon lose in enduring adolescence. It allowed me to feel the power of being the best. I would clutch my medal or trophy as the announcement of my name filled my head with an absolute sense of what I was: triumphant.

With adolescence, however, I became like so many other teenagers. In trying to become "the ideal," I became unlike myself, and I lost my athletic self. Adolescent ideals came into conflict with my childhood ideals like the crushing of bodies in a football game. American girlhood meant being demure and enticing, but sports had taught me the opposite virtues of competition and open aggression.

I still played sports, but not as actively. I understood somehow that being athletic wasn't so cool anymore, and it was even less cool to beat the boys. Athleticism seemed to have no place in my new world, and it certainly wasn't making me happy. It didn't give me the "right look" or a boyfriend. It seemed, quite simply, that nobody wanted to play anymore.

One of my most vivid teenage memories is of the day I rediscovered that early pride in being an athlete. Our referee in a high school girls' flag football game was the boys' football coach, who was well known for having coached O. J. Simpson in high school. Midway through the game he said to me in complete seriousness, "If you were a boy, I'd recruit you." On that day, I regained my belief in the value of athletic ability.

Several years later, I began doing farm work on a kibbutz in Israel. This period in which I indulged my natural inclination to physical labor was the first time I was truly happy since my tomboy days as a child. It felt good to become strong doing something physical. I felt I had finally "come home."

Compatibility with the land stretches back to our early physical instincts and the memory of our first major challenge: defying and overcoming the ground beneath us as we learn to walk. It continues throughout our early years, when we find pleasure in such earthy realities as dirt, trees, and the changing seasons.

An athlete I am; an athlete I was meant to be. I never strayed far from who I am, because I was always the same in the core of my being. Only the era or the circumstances changed, temporarily changing me or detouring me from my path.

Today I run, swim, lift weights or play tennis or shoot baskets, but mainly run: 50, 60, 70 miles a week. I began running ten years ago, but like most people, with no intention of competing. My interest in competition evolved with the popularity of road racing, and I began to race five years ago. Now I train to achieve, and I run races to test myself. Improving my best times of 37:36 for 10 kilometers and 63:30 for 10 miles is an important goal, but staying healthy and enjoying my running is the most important goal.

Physical pursuits remind us of the simplicity of life, and of the concrete relationships we have with the world. We long to be reminded of these things, to be relieved, even if only for a time, of the intangibles we encounter in our everyday lives, and our frequent feeling of an inability to control our destiny in a world of computers and politics.

In the physical universe we regain some semblance of control. As a farmer, I knew that what I harvested would be there tomorrow, and for many tomorrows afterward. I knew what would be produced. There is a sureness about our physical endeavors that is unduplicated in any other aspect of life.

As an athlete, I know what will happen to my body when I run. I know the point at which it will no doubt strain. I know my need for oxygen and from practice I learn to conserve it as best I can. I know that in a race there will be a point at which to begin, and one at which to finish, and that my movement between these two points is defined in minutes and seconds. Within those minutes and seconds an effort is needed that I know well. It is a lot to know, and I know it better than I know the stability of my job, my relationships with others, the state of affairs in troubled countries, or the likelihood of nuclear war.

I understand what it means to rediscover the athletic self, because like most of us I had lost it. When I lost my athletics and a sense of my physical self, I had lost my roots, and myself.

This is the self we all have, the one that longs to play games or run down the block—or the self that urges us to "put it on the line," to test ourselves in athletic competition.

Being an athlete does not necessarily mean being a champion, or even a competitor. It can mean jogging for fun or fitness, or playing ball or tennis. Being physical can be working in the garden or carrying piles of wood—anything that puts us back in touch with that innate instinct to use our bodies as vehicles of adventure, challenge, and discovery.

Above all, being an athlete is an attitude, a definition, a lifestyle choice. To proclaim by what we do and how we live that we are athletes is to say we believe in physical expression and the well-being it provides. For some of us it may mean a willingness to enter the world of competition in order to test ourselves, and to take from competition what is good. For others it may mean using physical resources for the first time.

A woman athlete makes an even more significant statement because she enters a world that heretofore has been closed to her. Athletics have traditionally been part of the male world, particularly off-limits to women because of their association with physical strength. But new doors are being opened to women, and behind these doors are new worlds. Sport is one of them.

We are blessed with amazing resources with which to live our lives, and the use of our bodies is one of the most important. It is a valuable endeavor to become physical again, to become an athlete. We can celebrate it. We can all find that which we have lost. We can rediscover our athletic self.

3

It's Okay
to Be Physical

No longer is sweating a sin
*Women Who Win**

THE MESSAGE being sent loud and clear in the eighties is that it's okay for women to be physical: to be aware of their own bodies, and to use them in new and more meaningful ways.

It's been a long evolution, beginning with the step-by-step reduction of confining clothing. From the shortening of floor-length skirts to the removal of corsets, clothing had gotten lesser and looser. The definition of female physical beauty has gone from the opposite extreme of the abundantly fleshy women of Peter Paul Rubens paintings to the look of today's slim and muscular models who even lift weights to get that way.

Gone are the days of pale, fragile beauty—the tubercular look of the Victorian days and the corsets so tight they rearranged a woman's inner organs. Even thin for thin's sake is out: dieting the flesh into shape is not enough; it has to be molded that way by exercise. Beauty is no longer passive, it's active, requiring that women take charge and create a look by choice, commitment, and hard work. So good-bye soft and fleshy, and hello slim and solid. Another female image bites the dust!

Critics of modern culture have accused society of putting too much emphasis on the body, and they are undoubtedly right. But we did not create this emphasis on physical appearance; we are merely responding to

*Parkhouse, Bonnie L. and Jackie Lapin. *Women Who Win: Exercising Your Rights in Sports.* New Jersey: Prentice Hall, Inc., 1980.

the world in which we live. We can either try to deny it, or accept it. We do have to feel good in our surroundings, because rail against society as we might, we still live within its bounds.

How can we fight this fixation on the body? Only when we possess something do we learn to understand it, and gain the freedom to put it in proper perspective. We have to be comfortable with our bodies (and ourselves) in order to be rid of a fixation on them. This is no small task, and disharmony with the body is not easily ignored. The great philosophers knew: split the mind from the body, and you split the personality. And it isn't just good looks that are the issue; it is a deeper physical ethic. There's a difference between body beautiful for its own sake and being an athlete.

Some feminists believe that the new standard of female beauty is just as oppressive as the old one. In proclaiming that "fat is a feminist issue," they hope to free overweight women from yet another social stereotype: the pressure to be thin.

There is no denying that one should always be free to choose, but accepting an overweight body is accepting a state of inferiority. A woman is giving up when she tells herself it is okay to be fat. Feminist author Letty Cottin Pogrebin takes issue with the fat is beautiful idea. She believes it means just taking up space in the world, a sign of ill-health and being out of control, and of passivity.

The rationale that it's all right to be fat and out of shape relieves a person of seeking and experiencing control over herself. And it is doubtful that it will make women happier, freer, or more functional to know they've beat the thin stereotype. I don't believe we ever beat an image, at least until we decide it has no value. I do believe there is that "thin" voice within us, and that it cries out against accepting an inferior state of physical conditioning, the result of a sedentary life. It is that voice that urges us to break bad habits and take control of ourselves, on all levels, because to accept a poor physical self is to accept a lesser self.

Of course, there is a goal between being model-thin and overweight. Learning to live with the reality of one's body *is* a feminist issue. However, a woman should accept her body when she has given her best effort to get in shape and feel good, when by her own power and ability she has made that body the best one it can be.

There's a lot to be said for heavy or out-of-shape women who are exercising, taking this control of their lives. It's more impressive to see them out running than to see a thin sedentary woman eating cookies and ice cream, complacent in her genetic predisposition. (She may not be getting away with much, anyway, as even thin people can have muscles and arteries laden with fat, making them prime candidates for the same diseases heavy people may suffer from.) Being fit is a feminist issue; it has to do with being strong and in control, not just being thin.

But getting fit may not be easy, because for many reasons we have ceased to be physical. In addition to a modern lifestyle that does not promote physical activity, our measure of worth in society is cerebral rather than physical ability. Physical activity has often been associated with lack of sophistication, and has even been considered as something primitive.

The sign of a modern woman's rise to success has been how well she performs in areas which have been male-dominated: business, corporate life—high-pressure desk jobs. So like men, the successful woman has been led away from her physical self. But a woman has been even more alienated, for not only is even less status associated with her sports or her physical life, but she is rebelling against *always* having been defined in physical terms—as either a "sex object" or a "baby maker."

Sex or babies, women believed, were all her body was meant for. It certainly wasn't meant to play football or hit home runs. Imagine the terrible paradox, then, for the young athletic girl, who in her innocence is shattered by her introduction to the adult female world for which she is so completely unprepared. On the one hand she has learned to perform as an athlete, but on the other, as a woman she is not intended to identify her body in athletic terms. She has not been prepared to continue her physically active life, which in turn would have enhanced her body's other values. Instead she is confused by the roles she is expected to fulfill. This dichotomy has plagued women for ages, even all the way back to those in the Victorian novels who often long for their girlhood romps on the seashore, and lament their adult female confinement.

The idea that being physically fit is merely "sexy" has its roots in the same sexism that has always made objects of women. If the only difference between the cover girls of the past and those of today is that the modern versions have muscles, athleticism is being exploited as a symbol of sexiness. Sexuality and a good body are undeniable benefits of being a fit and aware person, but they are not the sole reasons to be fit. They are positive side effects that enable women to develop a healthy body image.

It isn't that women runners aren't proud of their athletic looks, but it's doubtful they would be sweating, panting, and spitting during hard training runs and races if they hoped to be known for their physical beauty alone. They are athletes, not cover girls.

What does emerge of importance is that when a woman becomes body-defined, she comes into her own sexually. In her personal relationships, she is more likely to act than to be acted upon—and her new physical assertiveness gives her confidence in all other areas of life.

BECOMING BODY-DEFINED

Breathe, walk, move—and feel it happen. Do it often, with pride. It's a gift. Your awareness of your physical self is what it means to be body-defined. And conversely, every move you make—the way you walk, run, or stand—defines you. When you give a firm handshake, you are performing a physical gesture which conveys that you are strong, confident, and assertive. When you walk or run tall, with your full height, you exude confidence and charisma.

When you run, feel the air slide by. Run on the sand or the grass barefoot, and feel the ground. Look down at your feet—there are twenty-six bones in each of those feet! By becoming aware of your body, you take pleasure in all that you have. It's not narcissism; it's being alive!

Learn to feel your body through its activity. Learn to respect it by building a relationship with its components: bone, muscle, skin. When it works well, praise it. When it doesn't, try to understand why. The body is an intricate machine, but we are in awe of it not so much for its mechanical value, but for the miracles it performs for us.

When you get acquainted with your body, and work with it, you cease to be alienated from it. You cease to fear what has been foreign: blood, sickness, pain, physical labor—all the things that may have frightened you when you put no trust in your body, when you were like a stranger to yourself. Despite years of mythology and conditioning, women can be physically strong. We are not frail, though we may have been reduced to frailty. We are not physically weak by nature; it's just that most of us don't speak the language. But we're learning!

Exercise is a constructive act of giving to yourself. By exercising you enable yourself to feel and look good. An antithesis is dieting, which is an act of denial. Not only do you feel deprived, but dieting alone usually does not work. Of the 50 million Americans who are dieting, only 5 percent will maintain their weight loss.* According to experts, exercise together with a good diet is the winning combination.

Finally, if we can transcend the need to be physical for physical sake, and beautiful for beauty's sake—and when we can see through this shallow image that society perpetuates, women will be able to gain a deeper understanding of what it means to be body-defined. The need to watch ourselves in the mirror will become less important when we have learned to live with our bodies as ourselves rather than separate from ourselves.

*American Anorexia/Bulimia Association, Inc. Newsletter, Vol. VII, No. 1, January-March 1984.

How the body functions will become more aligned with the spirit rather than a reflection of surface beauty.

Being fit and being a runner is something a woman does for herself. Any comments from onlookers, whether lewd or complimentary, strike most women as insults and an invasion of privacy. They are not out running in order to display their bodies, or to have a conversation or be picked up on the run.

As women begin to identify more with the athletic values which have always been reserved for men, other stereotypes will be eradicated. One of these is the almost irrational fear some women have of being muscular. When women and exercise is the subject, we are constantly reminded not to worry, women's hormones won't allow them to develop ''bulging'' muscles like men. It seems a collective sigh of relief is then heard by both women and men everywhere. Even the pictures of the ''new athletic woman'' hoisting dumbbells usually feature ''safe'' poses which show no obvious musculature.

What's wrong with muscles, and having them? We love them on men, so why not love them on women? There are women who don't fear losing their femininity by becoming muscular, and why should they? It is a negative attitude to fear developing muscles, and we need to stop comparing women's muscles to men's, and be freed from the idea that there's something unfeminine about being muscular. The idea that a woman won't become as ''muscular as a man'' also implies she won't become as strong or as equal—in any and all respects. Women should be encouraged to go for it: to get as far, as fast, and as muscular as they can.

Far from being unfeminine, a strong body communicates a strong woman. I recently noticed two obviously fit and muscular women coming toward me on the street. They walked with long strides, the muscles in their legs quite visible. More noticeable were their striking good looks and the confident manner expressed by their movement. Men and women turned to look at them. If body language is any measure of rank, they no doubt belonged to royalty!

Few women athletes are ashamed of their bodies, and the more muscular the better. Athletic wear, shorts and sleeveless shirts, is skimpy for comfort, yet hordes of women don't hesitate to be seen in public in it. These are women who have paved the way for those yet to begin. So a newcomer need not feel she will turn into a man by engaging in sports when she has the model of millions of women who are already doing it.

It must be appreciated, however, that being in shape is hard work—no matter what the ads in the back of magazines promise about easy and instant fitness. The fitness we aspire to as athletes is not the easy kind, and this is precisely why it is so special to us. What we obtain is derived from the effort we give, just as in all facets of life. To hone the body, to run fast or long, takes time and effort, and the result of this effort is visible: top women runners look like top athletes.

This was illustrated in the case of Rosie Ruiz, who cheated in an attempt to win the 1980 Boston Marathon. In addition to the moral issue of the violation of fair play, she pretended to achieve athletic excellence without having worked for it. As I watched her ample rear end turn the last corner and head for the Boston Marathon finish line, it was her body that revealed she was a fake. Even male winner Bill Rodgers said to the press, "She couldn't have done it. She has too much fat on her."

I resented Ruiz because I identified with those women in the race who had worked hard for a true victory. Their bodies, showing evident signs of toil and struggle by the end of 26 miles, were in stark contrast to the relaxed look of the pretend victor.

There is no something for nothing. There is no instant fitness or solid and beautiful body. And this is how it should be; this is why we cherish our fitness, exactly because we have worked to attain it and made the choice to maintain it.

It is important to be physical, and even more important to understand the reasons why. More than just a fad, or the latest in good looks, it belongs to a deeper definition of oneself. It entails free and independent choice, and an investment of hard work—all of which affect the way we value ourselves and the world around us.

Today it is more than okay to be physical. It is a status which commands great respect, for yourself and from others. And whether you're muscular or rail-thin, just right or overweight-but-trying, you can become body-defined. You can become an athlete.

4

Why Run?

RUNNING IS EASY; we all know how to do it. It was one of the first things we learned. Even before we could talk we could run. It is a spontaneous activity and the basis for almost all childhood games. In fact, in the course of a day, children can run as much as five miles. When we run we are not beginning anew, but merely rekindling an old habit, one that's as easy as tying a pair of shoes and heading out the door. That's all you need—no expensive equipment, lessons, courts, or gyms. You can run anywhere—streets, parks, hills, and even stairways or mountains.

There are many reasons to begin running. First of all, it's an easy and enjoyable form of physical activity, and the results are the best proof of running's benefits. Secondly, it's an inherent skill; your accomplishment is immediate, and it takes little time to do. In terms of energy expenditure (i.e., the burning of calories), for the time invested in the exercise, running ranks at the top of the most popular sports for energy output, ahead of such worthy competitors as swimming, tennis, and bike riding.

These are some of the obvious benefits of any exercise program, and some of the more specific reasons to choose running. But there are even better reasons to join the thirty to forty million Americans who already run and who are part of a boom that is estimated will reach one in every three Americans by the end of the eighties. Why are we all doing it, and if you're not, why might you want to start?

Contrary to the belief that running is always stressful, it can in fact be quite relaxing. It's repetitive movement seems to calm us much the way rocking calms a baby, or having our hair brushed or our back stroked relaxes us. Dr. Robert Ornstein, a San Francisco research scientist, believes that the type of repetition in running actually has a calming effect on the central nervous system. In addition, it is widely believed that there are physiological reasons for the feelings of relaxation we derive through physical exercise. Running is said to release endorphins from the brain, opiatelike substances which act as tranquilizers.

Consider a daily run. It is usually an opportunity to put aside the worries and rigors of life. The mind downshifts from high gear, and we can do the activity automatically. We don't have to study or concentrate on how to put one foot in front of the other.

Dr. Ornstein has claimed that during exercise we operate with the right hemisphere of the brain, the intuitive side, versus the left hemisphere, which is involved in language, logic, and rational thought. In so doing, we allow the usually busy left side with which we function most of the day to rest or "idle."

Running is an act of wandering—in body, mind, and soul. On one level, it allows us a temporary escape from routine, and from the unpredictable or the difficult. It can also serve as a form of meditation, an opportunity to become centered. When we are completely involved in this one definable act—a literal moving forward on firm ground—we can achieve this centering, which is a focusing and an integration of ourselves. And just as we define our running by setting goals—deciding how far and how fast to go—running in turn defines us by the very process of doing it. In its Zen implications, running is complete and we are complete when we do it.

In support of its calming effect, running has been successfully used as a method of therapy with such groups as alcoholics, geriatric and psychiatric patients, and those suffering phobias. The California psychiatrist Thaddeus Kostrubala has documented his use of running as a treatment for anxiety, depression, and schizophrenia.

The New York Road Runners Club has brought running programs to drug rehabilitation centers, and presently conducts the Rikers Island prison running program for inmates and staff, both men and women. The program enables prisoners to develop a healthy physical outlet and creates a system of socialization with workouts and track meets.

If running can in fact relieve anxiety, a sizable population could use a pair of running shoes. According to Bahrke and Morgan in *The Psychology of Running*, anxiety is one of America's major health problems, affecting 2 to 4 percent of the general population, and an astounding 30 to 70 percent of those being treated by general practitioners for conditions caused by stress.

The growth in the number of people participating in sports, specifically running, which is the third most popular sport in America after bowling and swimming, represents a growth in our awareness of our need to be physically active and healthy. And the proliferation of group runs and races proves we need to test ourselves physically as we did in childhood, often against our peers.

We long to maintain that early and tangible involvement with our physical selves and the physical world around us. Running provides that physical relationship to a physical world. Foot after foot, on land, under sky: the act of running is done exactly, and in an exact framework. Its systems of measurement are equally precise: time and distance, which are finite gauges of our achievements. They require no personal judgment or special analysis to determine achievement, avoiding the possibility of judgments based on prejudice or whim. In the running world, there are no favorites who succeed with good looks or charm. Excellence is purely a result of ability.

The popularity of the sport and its discipline are partly a reaction to the hedonism of the sixties, which preached easy but ephemeral pleasure through free love, drugs, and a lifestyle symbolized by such deceased clichés as "letting it all hang out." Running represents control, preparation, discipline, and structure—the opposite virtues of the sixties life.

Particularly significant for women, running and sport symbolize a new physicality. Abundant, rounded flesh has been replaced by a new chic: fat is out; well-developed muscles and, in the extreme, even the appearance of a bone or two are in. Yet despite the current exaggeration of the importance of having an ideal body, striving to be trim and fit has helped promote a new sense of pride among women. The fact that millions of women every day go out for a run in shorts and a T-shirt is proof of a newfound body confidence.

If some don't favor the athletic look in women, it's probably due to nostalgia for the days of round, fleshy figures. Old images die hard. But as far as what is now desirable, there's hardly a woman runner who doesn't, or wouldn't, relish feeling firm and spare.

Running has created a new and refreshing social milieu as together women find a new commonality and camaraderie. As training partners they share personal goals, and learn to face one another as competitors in a race. In the athletic context, women relate differently not only to each other but to men as well.

It used to be that most men felt threatened by athletic women, and women athletes had to contend with the prejudice that put them outside the social mainstream. There was no in-between, either: a woman was a "jock" or she wasn't—with all the stereotypical associations attached to both roles. According to a recent survey of the American public, however, 84 percent say that participation in sports does not diminish a woman's femininity. Today men are more likely to be in admiration of athletic women, and women runners relate to men as both training partners and friends—a relationship of equals.

Women are taking up running in record numbers. According to the *Sporting Goods Dealer* 1983 sports census, there are 17.7 million women runners in the United States, and the number is rising. Statistics from the New York Road Runners Club, the largest running club in the world, with over 23,000 members, reveal that women's membership and participation in races have increased each year since 1982, while men's have stayed nearly the same.

Increased numbers have also spurred growth in the competitive area, in which there are greater opportunities for women in all categories. Statistics show that involvement of women in competitive running increased from 2 to 20 percent in the last five years. Most races now give awards in age-group categories in recognition of excellence on all levels, and for national and world-class runners, prize money purses and benefits are growing as fast as these elite women are running.

Running allows us an acceptable and healthy outlet for the competitive instincts we all have. For the majority of women who are unaccustomed to competitive athletics, the sport provides a noncombative activity, which is achievement-oriented rather than competition-oriented. On the roads we are all equal, and able to succeed on our own relative level. Because world champion Grete Waitz reaches the finish line while most of us are still in the middle of the race doesn't mean we don't go the same distance and undergo the same challenge and satisfaction from our effort. A race is not confined to the absolutes of winning or losing, but rather is significant for the goal of striving to perform to one's own potential. "Everyone is a winner" is the apt saying frequently applied to a road race.

Running embodies the feminist ideal of a woman achieving for herself, by herself, because in this sport, satisfaction and success are ultimately dependent on her. No aid, human or material, can give a woman what she gives herself when she sets and achieves her goals as a runner—from taking her first running steps to crossing the finish line. This self-sufficiency is a skill acquired for other aspects of life as well.

While running we escape the struggle for status, for in our shorts and T-shirts, or loose-fitting sweat suits, we display no obvious signs of wealth or rank. And there's less cause to feel self-conscious while running, with so many others doing the same thing, dressed the same way. On the roads or the track, the laborer can outrun the doctor, and the wealthy executive can be walloped by the struggling student. As a 1982 article on fitness in *Time* magazine points out, "The fit look has nothing elitist about it. It represents an attainable ideal for all ages, races, walks of life."* In clothing, habit, and manner, running offers what the rest of modern life cannot: simplification, not complication.

We're all running—slow or fast, fat or thin. And contrary to other popular exercise activities for women, running has almost nothing to do with the way we look when we do it. In many women's fitness routines the dependence on looks, grace, and performance still maintains the feminine mythology. Famous starlets may tell you that fitness is the basis of their exercise programs, but what you see is who best models the glitzy tights and the leotards that look as if they require surgery to get in and out of. In fact, it would probably serve most women well to be rid of the ubiquitous mirrors in gyms and health clubs, which detract from the most important reasons for getting in shape. Feeling good comes from within, and the only mirror that reflects that feeling is the one in the soul.

When women's fitness made the cover story of *Time* in August 1982, the introduction of the article applauded women who look great now that the "taut and toned" look is in. However, the article goes on to point out, "We've entered an age of mental and physical narcissism. Originally, man built a strong body to do work. Now women are building their bodies just to look good."

While narcissism is undeniably an element in the fitness movement, a distinction must be made between an image or trend and the personal meaning of sport to an individual woman. Of the nearly one thousand women runners surveyed in May 1983, at the L'eggs Mini Marathon in New York City, not one said that good looks were her main priority for engaging in the sport.

If the accusations of narcissism are true, women are faced with an unresolvable Catch-22. On one hand, they are surrounded by a slim, fit-loving world—emphasized in every designer-clothing and diet-soda commercial. Yet if they seek this ideal they are accused of being shallow and narcissistic. There is only one way to live in a world so full of contradictions, and that's to rewrite the rules of the game!

A strong body serves more than just looks. It feels right. It's more useful and productive than a weak body. It's not the look of bulging muscles that makes us feel good, it's what we do with them that gives us a sense of strength—whether in sports, lifting our own packages, or attain-

---

*"The New Ideal of Beauty," *Time*. August 30, 1982.

ing good posture as a result of being fit. Why shouldn't women want to be strong—just because they don't need to lift two-ton boulders from the land like their ancestors did?

Of course, running is not a panacea for all life's ills, nor will running or exercise solve life's problems or provide a ticket to nirvana. Much has been made of those who have used running, or other exercise, to an extreme. Let's not blame these excesses on running or sport, but rather on a society which habitually looks for an easy way out or an instant answer—whether it be through drugs, alcohol, or a pair of running shoes.

Our purpose should not be to dwell on the negative, but to extract what is good from running, and of that there is much. As in everything else, we learn through maturity and judgment to separate the bad from the good.

And so when sedentary onlookers ask you, "Why run?," the easiest answer is not an explanation of all the reasons, but an invitation to try it and find out for themselves.

5

When Running Changes Your Life

- Loretta Maloney began running five years after the birth of her fourth child when she was 39. "I was in a rut. I had no motivation staying around the house. I was used to working." Loretta recently began weekly speed workouts with a coach she met through her older daughter, a collegiate runner. She's already cut two minutes off her 5-km time.
- Isabelle Carmichael remembers that even as a child, "I always enjoyed beating people." She was athletic then, although she didn't begin jogging until she was in her late 20s and immediately showed signs of talent. However, her ability posed a threat to a jealous boyfriend. Three years ago she broke up with the boyfriend and took up serious running. At 33, she has qualified for the Olympic Marathon Trials with a time of 2:38:15.
- "I could see my life improving radically and steadily," says Angela Miller, who began regular running at age 30 after a series of personal difficulties. Today 36-year-old Angela is the head of her own publishing company and has completed two marathons and two triathlons.

These are three stories typical of the millions that describe women's running careers. And most are willing and anxious to talk about how and why they started running and how it has changed their lives. Because invariably, it has changed them. Whether by the loss of a few pounds, or a psychological sense of a new "high," women are saying that running means much more to them than the act of putting one foot in front of the other.

In the L'eggs Mini Marathon survey, women runners expressed various benefits of the sport: "Confidence. Time to be alone. Being taken seriously by men. Being in control. A feeling of self-importance, accomplishment, and individuality." The long list of praise continues, like the account of a new miracle drug.

Loretta Maloney was always athletic, and although she played basketball in high school, there were no women's sports teams when she was in college at Fordham in New York, where she received her degree in pharmacy. At 44 years old, with four children and a full-time job, Loretta possesses the type of achievement-oriented personality that seems to be drawn to running.

"I would come home high-strung and worn out after work," she recalls. "I started to run because of the encouragement of my husband, who's been doing it for twenty years."

Loretta first made the hour trip for speed-work sessions with her daughter, who is on a college track scholarship. When her daughter returned to school, however, Loretta continued going to the workouts on her own. "I've already improved my time in a 3.5-mile race from 32:40 to 30:46," she says of the sport she plans never to give up.

"Running helps work out all your problems and prevents depression. I come back revived and more alive after a run. It uplifts my spirits." Loretta admits she doesn't mind the added benefit of keeping her weight down. "Running is like going on a diet, but so much easier!"

Isabelle Carmichael looks nothing like a "born again" athlete. In fact, she looks like she's never been anything but an athlete. At 5 feet 4½ inches and 105 pounds of solid muscle, she has a classic runner's body.

Isabelle toyed with running in the late seventies, improving her marathon time of 3:29 to 3:04 on only five months of light running. During this time, she says, "I got over any shyness of shorts and spitting." However, there remained another serious problem for her. Involved in a bad relationship with a man who was very competitive, she became emotionally and physically worn out attempting to juggle his needs with her growing desire to fulfill her own.

In the last three years, Isabelle has made radical changes in her life and come to some radically new conclusions. She dropped her boyfriend and took up serious running. Her goal now is to fulfill her potential as a runner. To do so she says she must be single-minded and focus on her mental discipline. "I've been told that I have the combination of physical attributes it takes to be a good runner; any doubts I have are more with my emotional or mental strength."

Meanwhile, in addition to her full-time job in marketing, Isabelle has run races in Russia, Sweden, Guatemala, and around the United States. If it were not easy to understand her devotion to running, it became clearer on September 3, 1983, at the Fifth Avenue Mile. Before 50,000 fans, a smiling Isabelle Carmichael broke the tape in 4:48 to win the metropolitan division of the race. As she stood on the victory platform, hoisting a silver tray above her head, her beaming smile radiated the entire length of the avenue.

Angela Miller began running on and off at age 24 in order to lose weight after the birth of her daughter. By age 29, after a divorce and other family crises, she felt overwhelmed. "I wanted to do something alone— away from the problems. After college, a marriage, and a baby, I felt lost. I wanted control of my life. A serious running program somehow gave me back that feeling of control."

After two years of "mile after mile on my own," Angela finally entered a race. On the starting line she was filled with a sudden panic. "How could an 'aging,' divorced mother race?!" she thought. But she did, and in the final mile she began to cry. "I'm going to do it!" she said to the uncomprehending masses around her. They could not have known how much it meant to her to start and finish that race. But she understood.

For a time, running became an all-consuming passion for her, but today Angela has it more in perspective. "I don't have to talk about it so much anymore. It's part of my life. And my self-esteem has recovered from the bruising it took." Running still allows her to enter another world, "where everyone is stripped to nothing—credentials don't matter." She enjoys this escape from the world of book publishing. "I have to get out to run to regain control. I want a healthy body and a healthy mind, and if I don't run, they both suffer."

For most women the changes that result from running are more than just healthy; they can be downright life-giving. Running does change lives, often radically. Yet sometimes the change is not for the good. As the numbers of women running increase and as women's athletics becomes an ambitious pursuit, there are bound to be some lives negatively affected.

One of the most common ailments for those who begin to take running seriously is burnout. A prime characteristic of distance runners is compulsion, and when this compulsion is coupled with a woman's sudden discovery that she can run well and achieve a new level of self-esteem, it makes her prone to all the problems of excess. Burnout can be physical or mental, but it's usually some of both. It can result in exhaustion, injury, and a forced vacation from the sport which was once a way of life.

Her story is well known in the running world. In an amazingly brief few years, Patti Catalano had gone from sedentary smoker to American record holder in almost every distance from 5 miles to the marathon. Under her husband's coaching, she ran as much as 150 miles a week, with three weight-lifting sessions. She raced frequently and successfully, ate enormous amounts of food to keep herself fueled, and talked with tremendous enthusiasm about her newfound life as a runner.

By 1981, however, Catalano had suffered a series of disappointments caused by injuries, which were followed by difficulties in her marriage. Without her success in running, she had lost her sense of self-worth and was forced to reevaluate her life and her goals. Her weight shot up, but she managed to salvage her marriage. It's been several years since she ran a race in her old form, and at last report she is still working to make a comeback.

Dana Slater is a national class runner and winner of the world-famous São Paulo midnight run two years in a row. Yet her natural running ability has never been motivation enough. Introspective and wise beyond her 24 years, Dana was perhaps almost too analytical about her running. The intensity of her life in the sport finally forced her to quit. The pressure, and the pain, were more than she could take on a continual basis. But each time she quit, a nagging doubt would remain.

When Dana transferred to the University of Virginia in her junior year and joined the track team, she thrived on the camaraderie of one of the nation's top collegiate teams. In 1982, she was a member of the University of Virginia cross-country team, which won the National Collegiate Championship and the TAC/USA National Championship—the only team ever to score victories in both these meets in the same year. After that season, Dana stopped competing. This time, however, she claims she is happy to have retired after a positive experience, and after getting what she wants from the sport. She still runs, rides her bike, and plays rugby, but it's all for fun.

"When the fire goes out, it's time to leave the sport," says Dana. "It can't be a carefree activity if you want to be good or great. You have to have a more professional attitude. I wish I had the fire, because it was a good time when I was competing. It can open so many doors. You learn so much about yourself, and about others."

Serious running is not without its risks. There is often a delicate balance between athletic excellence and disaster, negotiated especially by those who have thrown themselves into the pursuit of running with such total devotion.

But the majority of women runners do manage to keep the sport in perspective, and the testimony of millions of them, most of whom have discovered the joys of sports for the first time, proves that whatever the changes in their lives have been, they have usually been for the better.

6

Running Relationships

HE WAS AIMING to make the Olympic team for his country—a once-in-a-lifetime obsession—and then it would be over. Then we'd settle down; then the hustle from track meet to road race, from city to country, would end. Then it would be my turn to pick a place to live and we would make more permanent plans.

First it was the Montreal Olympics in 1976. But when he barely missed qualifying, it became Moscow in 1980 and four more years. When his country boycotted, it was Los Angeles in 1984. For five years the obsession continued, and there was always a dream, a goal that required his complete devotion.

I never saw the end of the dream, the Olympics, or the chance to get "my turn," because in 1979, three months before running yet another marathon for another qualifying time, he left me. "I want to live alone," he calmly announced, and five years of his dream became no more to me than a bit of dust. Although I had been a recreational runner who loved the sport and the excitement of top track meets, it now made me tired. I had been used and tossed away, and suddenly life in the world's running capital of Oregon meant nothing.

Two years later, and still just as obsessed by more qualifying times and more dreams, he came to my new turf to run the New York City Marathon. Meanwhile, I had begun to train and run races (it was finally, ironically, "my turn") and knocked several minutes off my times.

We jogged down the street and stopped at a red light. Expecting my old pace, he was breathing audibly. "When did you start to run so fast?" he asked with a smile. With bitter, undisguised anger, I turned to him and said, "Didn't it ever occur to you that I could be a runner too?" "No, not really," he answered with the same casual candor that had once sliced my heart in two. But no more.

Like countless others, I too have been the victim of an unsuccessful running relationship. My tendency, like most others, is to attribute the problems to other factors, of which there are many. But the statistics on running relationships are telling. Although certainly not all of them fail, according to an article in *Running Times* magazine the divorce rate is three times higher among runners than the national average, and a New York City Marathon survey showed it is 340 percent higher than the rate among nonrunners.

A study of 250 runners and their spouses by family therapist Chris Shipman revealed that the best relationships consisted of two runners. Male runners married to sedentary females had only a 50-50 chance of overcoming difficulties, while the worst situation existed between running women and sedentary men. Significantly, women runners were twice as likely as male runners to reassess their relationships due to their sport.

Although the causes of divorce are infinitely more complicated than an hour or two a day spent pounding the roads, there are aspects of running which may possibly contribute to the decay of personal relationships. It may be likely that the high breakup rate among runners has something to do with the narcissism and the self-absorption which are the nature of the sport. Running is by definition a singular and private endeavor. A less severe analysis is that some cannot make the significant adaptation that is needed by both partners to an activity which will automatically in some way exclude one from the other, even if they both run. Sports psychology specialist Linda Lewis Griffith confirms that for all these reasons there's a lot of divorce involving women athletes because it's hard to maintain a marriage while competing in sports.

In my case, it isn't difficult to see: I confused devotion to a goal with a personal obsession. Worst of all, I misdirected my own love of sport into another person's life instead of focusing on it in my own. Not a day goes by when I don't curse myself for living someone else's dream, and failing to dream one of my own.

The couple in which the male is a top runner and the woman is on the sidelines is like the men who wage war while the women sit home and knit and worry: it's standard. But what about the couple where the woman gets good and the man can't take it? Shipman's study showed that sedentary men were jealous of their athletic wives, and whereas women runners sought athletic partners, most male runners said it was unimportant whether their wives ran. There is still that stubborn, persistent belief that a woman's excellence is like a gun pointed directly at the target of a man's ego.

Coupled with the fear of being outdone is the milieu in which it happens. Sports is almost the last frontier, the strongest bastion of male identity and power. Beat a man on the turf that has always been his, and the true test of equality begins. When the dust of battle settles, however, the male world may find that there was never even a fight, because the woman runner by virtue of her sport has already achieved independence. She may never need to fight that same battle again.

Once again, the evidence proves it. In a Kansas State test of 121 champion women track performers, it was found that they scored high in asceticism—the capacity for self-discipline and self-denial. Therefore they are better able to find satisfaction in intense training, effort, and competition. Perhaps this explains why some data indicate that a higher percentage of female runners than male runners are single. "The change in my life had a lot to do with running," says veteran woman distance runner Nina Kuscsik, who has raised three children on her own since 1973. "I explored myself with more confidence. It made me recognize what I had in my marriage."

Several explanations of the potential hazards of running on relationships have been well documented. A common one is that the activity takes time and attention away from spouses and families. Another interpretation is that the confidence and independence gained through running give people the ability and courage to analyze the choices they have made, and marriage may be one of the most vulnerable. Additional stress on the relationship is caused by the fact that most runners are married to nonrunners, and someone has to be fairly adaptable, or fairly mellow, to understand and accept a typical runner's obsession.

Linda Schreiber, a housewife and mother of five (including quadruplets), began running nine years ago, and achieved fame not only from her book *Marathon Mom*, but from her sub-3-hour marathon ability. Her running, which initially pleased her husband, eventually became the focal point of their divorce. After informal interviews with many separated or divorced runners, she concludes, "It isn't running per se that causes the breakdown of a marriage. The runner who divorces usually brings a troubled marriage to his or her running in the first place." This is probably true, but when Schreiber herself became increasingly involved in her own pursuit, which took more and more of her time and energy, her husband slowly withdrew his once enthusiastic support of her running. They were separated within a month after the publication of her book.

While running may require adjustment within personal relationships, it may also create greater stability. Running may break a relationship apart; on the other hand, it may also teach the very qualities found in stable, successful partnerships: commitment, discipline, and tenacity. A runner learns through sport what he or she must bring to life: adaptability, toughness, and humility. While some suspect the runner is a person seeking to become unglued from reality, there is in fact much evidence that fitness results in increased emotional stability.

Can "Stand by Your Man" be switched to "Stand by Your Woman"? "Only a certain kind of man can be Mr. Billie Jean King, watching the woman in the limelight," points out Linda Lewis Griffith. But there are men who not only adapt, but support the achievements of their running wives. Says Grete Waitz, "I'm very happy I'm married to Jack because he's very interested in my running. He wants to help me as much as he can. Sometimes I really admire a woman for instance who is married to a man who doesn't support her, who's not interested in running at all, and she goes out and trains ten or twelve times a week. I couldn't do it without the support of my husband." Women's distance running would not be what it is today if Jack Waitz hadn't repeatedly encouraged his wife to run her first marathon back in 1978.

When Charlotte Teske of West Germany began running at 18 years of age, her husband encouraged her to go for it. "Try to run more; try to train more seriously," he urged her. Today the 33-year-old Teske is the women's West German national record holder in the marathon, a former Boston Marathon winner, and ranks in the top ten in the world among women with her time of 2:28:32. Her husband, who is also her coach, escorts her on long runs on a bicycle. "He knows me every day," stresses Charlotte, "when I feel fit, when I feel tired. If you are on a high performance level, you need a coach you can trust, who you can talk to every time you want to—night or day." Charlotte realizes the solitary nature of her running, as well as the importance of her relationship with her coach/husband. "I train for myself, but if I have problems, I can say to my husband, 'Hey, can you help me; can we talk about it?'"

A significant number of women runners end up in romantic relationships with their coaches, many of which culminate in marriage. The coach seems to be the one person who can understand. Linda Lewis Griffith says that one of the biggest problems for the woman athlete is that she feels alone. "I was used to being an oddball," says Nina Kuscsik of her days as a lone woman marathoner. "It was an extension of not fitting into this world." In addition, often a woman will rely on a coach more than a male runner because she has not been conditioned to take a leadership role herself.

One of the best-known coach/athlete running relationships is that of Joe and Patti Catalano. Standing on the sidelines of the New York City Marathon one year, Patti was in awe of Grete Waitz as she came in under 2:30. Coach Joe told then 2:40 marathoner Patti Lyons, "You're going to do that one day." Several years later, Patti Catalano, a 2:27 marathoner, would repeatedly credit her coach and husband Joe with her success. Undoubtedly she remembered back to the day when he predicted her future, and then made it come true.

Doreen Ennis was 14 years old when she began running and when she met her first and only coach, John Schwarz. She went on to become the Junior National and Collegiate National 1500-meter champion, and a multi-time Olympic trials qualifier. At age 27, she qualified for the Olympic marathon trials in 1984.

During all these years, Doreen didn't have much time for social activities because of her running, which was the most important thing in her life. No high school proms. No dates. No boyfriends. The stability of her relationship with her coach was so important to her that she turned down a full scholarship to national track-power UCLA in order to attend Montclair State, a local New Jersey college where she could remain with John as her coach.

After Doreen graduated from high school, John asked her and her parents how they would feel if he dated her. Although romance had never occurred to her, she had built the beginnings of a lifetime of respect for him. "I had always considered him like an older brother. I looked up to him and respected him because of his knowledge and ability." Doreen says she realized the pros and cons of dating—that she'd have to separate the romance from the coaching. "He was better at it than I was," she says. "He could yell at me during practice, and then call the same night and ask me for a date."

In 1981, they were married. Says Doreen, "You can't help but get close; you're with the person so much. We had so much in common—the same values, the same interests. He'd understand if I was too tired to do something, if I didn't want to go out."

Just as Doreen the runner needed someone to understand her sport, John, a coach since age 18, needed someone to understand his interest and profession. Now 32 and a high school coach in addition to coaching Doreen, John remembers old girlfriends who would get upset when he would have to go home early for the next day's track meets. "It's important that the person I'm with understand what I'm doing," he says in partial explanation of his attraction to Doreen.

John feels that the only problem with his role is that it's often difficult to wear the two suits of husband and coach. "It's a problem switching roles. It'd be easier for the running perhaps if we weren't married. There would be more objectivity."

Certainly a coach/athlete relationship is potentially difficult, as it is by definition partly a relationship of unequals. The coach is the teacher, older brother figure, the superior. In fact, paralleling a father figure, in many coach/athlete relationships the coach is significantly older than the athlete.

One woman who has achieved running success and romance with her coach of three years says she sometimes fears that his judgment of her competition on the roads spills over to her life after the race. "I let you down," she once told him after a bad race, and it was hard to separate the comment from life in general. Sometimes, for some women, there may be more at stake than winning or losing a race.

But the attraction is obvious. A woman like the runner above, who is in her 30s, finds a man who encourages her athletic interests and helps her in succeeding in a way parents, friends, and peers may never have done. And the coach knows his role: he's not there to compete with his girlfriend, as so many of her past companions may have done. The two parties speak the same language, and it's a language that is rarely spoken, or even understood, by others.

Sometimes it works; sometimes it fails, but the pain of failure is universal. What about when it's the man who buries his career for the woman, and a running career at that? Can the running shoe be on the other foot? "I'm Ron Tabb again instead of Ron Decker," says the ex-husband of world-renowned distance runner Mary Decker, who is also one of the fastest American male marathoners with a time of 2:09:31. For the twenty-two months of their marriage, Tabb could be seen in the middle of the track, holding Mary's warm-up suit and encouraging her. When it was over, the running world knew that Ron Tabb was wounded. "When you're putting that kind of energy into someone else's career, yours is going to suffer," he eventually admitted. He went on to go from supposed has-been to second place in the Boston Marathon, a spot on the World Championship team, and third place in the New York City Marathon. "My improvement has a lot to do with my personal situation," he acknowledged.

Are we, either men or women, to give up individual drives and goals in order to blend into a successful partnership? Surely we can maintain an independence which allows each of us our own aspirations. Strong partnerships, like strong bodies, can accommodate great stress—healthy stress—and adapt and grow. Despite all the difficulties, which are no doubt the same in any relationship in which one or both parties are driven by ambitions and dreams, there are success stories like Grete Waitz, Charlotte

Teske, and Doreen Ennis. And if the woman with total devotion to running can be part of a successful relationship, surely it is a good sign for any woman who takes up the sport.

Undoubtedly, running does not a marriage make, or break. And a running relationship *can* work, if a balance is struck. People must perhaps be more accommodating of each other, make some statements and decisions, and learn to deal with the same change and element of surprise that can happen anywhere, at any time, in any way. One learns not to decide in absolute terms, not to say always, or never—which was what I said about the possibility of ever getting involved with a runner again. Never.

I am now married to a man who has been running over 100 miles a week since high school, and ran his best marathon in 1980 when he came in fifth in Boston. He dreams of becoming a professional runner, and aspires to it every time he steps out the door to train. But those aspirations do not exclude or consume all others, nor do they blind him to the rest of life in the world.

Running is a large part of his life, as it is a large part of mine—but it's separate. Although we share the lifestyle of athletes and the love of the sport, we almost never run together. It is not of mutual benefit or interest. He runs with other men of his own ability, and I train with runners of my ability. His running is his individual dream, and my running is mine. But when the door is shut behind us after a workout, and the shoes are put in the corner where many pairs are piled high, life must, and does, go on to other things.

7

Running for Young Girls

A TRUE STORY

A class of children is running a loop of a large grass field, striding awkwardly and desperately in their street clothes. The heavier and less physical children are dropping further and further back as they approach. From a distance one can see the contrast with the leader: the fluid stride of a tall, slender girl with her hair drawn back in a rhythmically bouncing ponytail.

The group passes. Those in the back have begun to chat in a gesture of relinquishing the lead, and the activity. The girl in front lengthens her stride, and pulls further away.

As she draws near, her expression reveals that she is not straining in the slightest, and she smiles as if to show she is doing what comes naturally, from a place she belongs: the lead.

Every woman who runs has had the fantasy, for herself or perhaps her daughter. She has felt, or wanted to feel, like the girl who runs gracefully ahead of her class: a being apart, blessed, set free by her movement and her talent. The dream, which begins with the discovery of a love of sport, or a hidden talent, grows to championship proportions: What if I had started younger? What if my daughter begins now?

Running for young girls can be a tremendous asset. For proof, one need only consider such a phenomenon as South African teenager Zola Budd, who at 5 feet 3 inches, 84 pounds, and 17 years of age strode in her bare feet to a women's world record time for 5,000 meters in January,

1984. In a study of high school student athletes, it was found they had a much more positive body image than nonathletes. In fact, they actually rated themselves equally or even more feminine than the nonathlete high school students.

However, with few exceptions, the women who today win races and hold the running records were not like the girl in the story, or in our fantasies. They were not running laps at age 3, or breaking finish tapes as skinny adolescents. And although the opportunities exist for women runners of all ages, the stars of tomorrow are probably not the child sensations of today.

"It's very seldom that the runners who are good when young will be good when they're older," says Grete Waitz, the star of women's distance running. "I think they get tired of it. When I started, I wasn't particularly good until I was fifteen or sixteen." The world-class career of 2:26 marathoner Julie Brown didn't begin until she took up regular running at 18. Joan Benoit, who didn't begin running until high school and ran an undistinguished fourteenth place in the National Junior Cross Country Championships at age 18, set her marathon world record at age 25.

Children run so naturally and look so good that it seems obvious they were born to do it, but there can be a big difference between children's spontaneous and natural running and how adults interpret their ability.

Regular distance running for children has raised concern for the possible risks of heat injury, joint and bone injuries, knee and heel problems, and Osgood-Schlatter's disease (a form of tendinitis in the knee). Further concern has been raised over studies that indicate young athletic girls experience puberty at a later age than nonathletic girls, and are prone during adolescence to iron deficiency.*

Perhaps the greatest yet most intangible damage is the possible psychological trauma caused by the pressure to perform or compete. Unfortunately, the Little League syndrome of pushy parents and anxiety-ridden youngsters is alive and thriving in the running world.

Several years ago I was midway through a 5-mile race when I noticed a smoothly striding young girl of about 11. Her talent was obvious to everyone, especially the crowds, who cheered her enthusiastically. As I went by her, I heard a desperate loud cry and saw her push aside the male runners who separated us. She forged ahead with phenomenal determination—too much determination, I realized. I became more and more uncomfortable passing her—each time I did, I heard her let out a cry. Down the homestretch a man who I later found out was her father yelled, "Let

*The Physician and Sports Medicine, vol. 11, no. 6, June 1983.

her win!" I had been contemplating doing just that, but the comment made me realize that "giving" a victory to her, or anyone, was the wrong thing to do. I drove by her to the finish line. As I turned to congratulate the budding star who could obviously outrun me in a matter of time, her eyes fluttered high in their sockets and she fainted.

The experience was devastating, and I took my concern to New York Road Runners Club president Fred Lebow. We discovered that week after week, the girl's father, even against the wishes of a top coach, brought her to races of up to a half marathon. After all of them she passed out.

Partly as a result of my experience in that 5-mile race, that year the New York City Marathon placed a minimum age limit of 16 on all entrants. "We can't be sure of the physical effects of children running a marathon, but the possible psychological and emotional damage should surely be avoided," concluded Lebow. The Committee on Sports Medicine for the American Academy of Pediatrics concurs. The committee thought that children should not engage in long-distance competitive running events primarily designed for adults, and that youths should not attempt a full marathon.*

Avon women's running director Kathrine Switzer expresses a similar philosophy. "Our experience with children in long-distance running, particularly ten miles or more, has been very negative—not only in terms of fatigue and low performance levels of the children, but more alarmingly, the relentless pressure from children's parents, which we clearly believe has often been psychologically abusive." Avon's marathon age restriction is 14 in keeping with the policy of the Women's Long Distance Running Committee of The Athletics Congress (TAC), which sanctions championship races (10 km to marathon) only for ages 14 and over.

This doesn't mean running isn't good for children, or that it shouldn't be encouraged. There are appropriate races of appropriate distances for children. However, their running should be done in moderation, keeping in mind that the aim of participation is enjoyment and development of fitness in childhood that, according to experts, greatly affects adult fitness.

John Babington has been the distance coach of the Boston-based women's running team Liberty Athletic Club since 1974. He trains many a young girl among the club's 125 runners. Although he avoids a highly structured training program for the younger runners and does not hesitate to come down hard on parents who push their children, he finds a discouragingly high percentage of young girls who eventually have motivational problems during their running careers. "I've asked myself often if it

*"Is Running For Children?" *The Health Letter*, May 27, 1983.

wouldn't have been better for some of these girls to start at 18. Yet when they arrive as at my doorstep—active, motivated—I can't squelch their enthusiasm. I don't want to keep them out of running, and I'm idealistic enough to believe that they *can* have a lifelong running experience."

Babington's guidelines come from his years of coaching experience, and his take-it-easy approach has cultivated such runners as world marathon record holder Joan Benoit, and multi-time national mile champion Darlene Beckford. A 12-year-old Liberty AC-er runs only an average of 3 miles a day. "No more," stresses Babington. "Through evolution it will increase." A 13-year-old is held at 3 to 5 miles a day, and a high school senior's upper limits are 6 to 7 miles. Despite acknowledging the controversy over young girls running hard, Babington believes there's nothing wrong with it, and includes two sessions a week of "some kind of speedier running."

"Too much intense competition at a young age will detract from enthusiasm," concludes Babington. As far as he's concerned, the perplexing problem of runner's burnout is not physical, but strictly emotional.

There's a difficult transition time for a girl. "If she starts running before physical maturity, at ten to twelve, it's effortless, and she's a perpetual motion machine. But after puberty when the percentage of body fat increases, it's harder. She will have to undergo more difficult training, and on an adult level."

The running boom may have changed things slightly, Babington admits, but not much. "Right from the start I found women to be legitimately competitive athletes. And I've seen every variation of competitiveness, all the way to top runners like the Welch twins, who punch on a wall before a competition to get themselves tough. I never get a noncompetitive athlete who says, 'I just love to run.'"

If the running boom has not affected the basic personality of the competitive girl athlete, it has effected change on the masses of girls and women taking up the sport. The number of colleges giving women's track and field scholarships has more than doubled in the past five years, and high school participation has soared 532 percent over the past decade.* There are now over 500,000 participants in women's high school track and field, making it the third most popular high school sport.† The 1983 Colgate Women's Games in New York City, the world's largest women's track and field meet, drew 22,000 competitors,‡ almost all of whom were young

*Gloria Averbuch, "The New Female Runner Is a Trained Competitor," *The New York Times*, May 23, 1982.
†"Sports Participation Survey Indicates Overall Increase," *Press*, vol. 2, no. 2, Oct. 1981.
‡The Softness Group, public relations firm for the Colgate Women's Games.

girls. The number of young girls running could be a significant future trend. In a Gallup Youth Survey taken in late 1983, 55 percent of American teenagers said they jogged, and participation by females (57 percent) has now surpassed males (54 percent).*

Though not all youngsters are meant to be competitors, most can gain the recreational benefits of running and can develop an important foundation for the lifelong enjoyment of sports. Milena Krondl of the New York Road Runners Club remembers the pain of not being allowed to join the track club in her native Czechoslovakia because she wasn't fast enough for the selective Eastern European system. Today she is the director of the Urban Running Program, a system of workouts and low-key races for children in all five boroughs of New York. The program emphasizes participation, says Krondl, and is designed for children who aren't necessarily competitive. In addition, it's held almost all year long, as opposed to the occasional children's race. Coaches in the program who discover talent and motivation refer children to track clubs. Several young girls from the Urban Running Program have already joined competitive teams, and one has achieved national ranking.

So what do you do to share your interest in running? "If I had a daughter," speculates Grete Waitz, "I would try and get her interested in running, but never push her if she didn't want to run. You have to enjoy what you're doing. I know from experience, as my parents pushed me into taking piano lessons, which I hated."

According to Grete, one can assume that if she had been like the young girl crying and fainting in road races, she wouldn't be the world's most famous distance runner at age 30. On the other hand, as John Babington points out, you can't squelch a young runner's enthusiasm.

The best you can do is to become a role model—showing it's okay to be female and active. After all, psychologists claim that although there are clear differences between baby boys and girls, it's how they're socialized that really determines their interests and personality.

Gentle encouragement, common sense, and guidance are the key for parents who want to help their children run. Whether a young girl grows up to become a champion, or just a fun runner, is up to fate. Either way, she'll come out a winner.

*"Half Americas Teenagers Jog," *Running Time*, April 1984.

8

Running After Forty
and Beyond

R UNNING IS ONE of the sports most compatible with age. It requires a skill which does not necessarily diminish with the years, and which can in fact improve. It also provides an opportunity for almost everyone to achieve fitness, stay in touch with her body, and maintain a healthy psychological outlook on life. The health-conscious lifestyle that usually accompanies running also provides a way of helping people control their destiny, so that age need not simply be a waning of health and life. The older woman runner can become the mistress of her fate.

Running into age is also beneficial for medical reasons. Exercise keeps calcium in the bones, protecting against osteoporosis (bone loss). It is also helpful in reducing the risk of heart disease and other problems associated with overweight in older women, such as diabetes, gallbladder disease, gout, and certain cancers. Norepinephrine, a hormone that promotes alertness but decreases with age, increases with exercise, as do endorphins—tranquilizing and mood-elevating substances.

Dr. George Sheehan, who believes running into age allows a 60-year-old to live in a 30-year-old body, quotes statistics from a study done of endurance racers showing only a 7 percent reduction in performance for every decade of age past their prime. Another study showed that given a suitable training program, the sedentary 69-year-old can improve by the same percentage as the sedentary 28-year-old. Considering the accomplishments of master's runners (the category for over 40), it seems there is every reason to believe that athletic ability can prosper with the years.

Take Joyce Smith, for instance. At age 27, she was an Olympic medalist in the 1500 meters. At 46, this English mother of two is one of the fastest woman marathoners in the world and has run two 2:29 marathons, one of only a handful of women in history to break 2:30 more than once. She finished ninth in the first World Championships marathon, fifth in the 1983 Avon International Women's Marathon, and could possibly represent her country in the 1984 Olympic marathon.

Or consider Cindy Dalrymple. The mother of two teenage sons, in 1974 after a ten-year lay-off Cindy resumed the sport she had taken up in college. For years she has logged 100 to 140 miles a week, high mileage for any elite woman or man, and remarkably has never been injured. She holds the American master's record in the 10 kilometers (34:40) and the 15 kilometers (54:44), and the second-fastest marathon of 2:43 (her career best is 2:39, which she ran at age 39). At 5 feet 9 inches, 130 pounds, and the overall women's winner in many races, Cindy is still running personal best times, and shows no signs of slowing down.

Granted, Joyce Smith and Cindy Dalrymple are in a class by themselves—exceptions not only among women their age, but among all women who run. They are on an elite level regardless of age, and these days can earn a living from the benefits of race awards money and promotions. But what about the average woman over 40?

According to a series of studies on older women runners begun in 1979, 90 percent said that running made them feel more comfortable with aging. "People are taking up running partly as a refusal to give in to getting older," confirms top master's runner Elaine Kirchen.

Kirchen also claims that the sedentary 40-year-old "is facing bulges a runner does not face" and thinks a primary reason for taking up the sport is weight consciousness. If this is so, the study on older women runners confirms it's working: half of the women over 30 questioned had lost at least 10 pounds.

Other findings of the study included the following:

- After becoming runners, most of the women greatly reduced their consumption of sugar and meat.

- Older women runners were sick less often than younger runners.

- Fewer of the older runners experienced amenorrhea (cessation of menstruation).

- Elite marathoners were depressed more often than non-elite marathoners, but far less often than nonrunners.

One finding was of significant psychological and social importance. Whereas runners in their 30s perceived the benefits of the sport as primarily physical, the 40–59 group, although placing importance on the physical benefits, saw running more as an adventure—"an exciting new experience."

Coach John Babington, whose Liberty AC master's team is the best in New England, seems to find the same attitude of excitement among his runners. "They've got a new and youthful approach, and an enthusiasm like teenage kids." Yet Babington's "kids" are just as serious, and able, as the rest of the runners in his club. Barbara Pike, who placed second among 40- to 44-year-olds in the World Master's Championships in Puerto Rico in the 1500 meters, runs a 5:12 mile.

Babington's master's runners up to their 50s race all distances, including marathons. They run up to 70 miles a week in training, and although they may do fewer speed workouts, the sessions are not different from those of his younger athletes.

Elaine Kirchen, a runner in her early 40s and a member of New York's Warren Street club, breaks all the rules, however, and not just for a master's runner, but for any human being. Up at 5 a.m., she puts in 10 miles running and 10 miles biking before heading to her job as an executive recruiter, at which she excels in a high-powered world which few women inhabit. After work she swims for an hour, and then goes out with friends. "Being tired," claims Elaine, "is a waste of time."

Contrary to a dread of turning 40, Elaine ordered her own birthday cake on which she joyously inscribed, "Good-bye Sub-Vets!" ("Sub-Vets" is the race category for 30- to 39-year-olds). Age has been good to her. She ran her second marathon in 2:48:34, which qualified her for the women's Olympic marathon trials, and was the third fastest by an American master and an improvement by 16 minutes over her first marathon.

Says Elaine, "The younger women I compete against may have younger bodies, and the benefits of college training, but I won't let age be my excuse." Despite her superior accomplishments, she claims, "I don't have any gifts. I'm nobody special, and nothing was given to me that was not given to other people." She believes her achievement is a matter of her willingness to devote the time to training, and she has always been directed, and "terribly competitive."

Elaine handles her sudden running success with a Zen-like calm. "My goal is to live day to day, and live every day fully." If it sounds all easy, it isn't. She had a rough spell when she began running in the seventies to escape the pain of a bad marriage. "I used to hate myself," is how she says she felt. Today she thoroughly enjoys life, and says she was "thrilled to run the Olympic Trials, and compete with people who are on the Olympic team."

50s Toshiko D'Elia crossed the finish line of her first race in good form to the sound of her daughter's incredulous shouts. "Oh my God, it's my mother!" she wildly cheered. Toshiko was 44 years old, and she wasn't far behind her own daughter. She went on to become the first 50-year-old woman to break the 3-hour barrier in the marathon with a stunning 2:57:25, which she ran in 1980. She is quick to acknowledge, however, that Sister Marion Irvine, a 54-year-old nun from California, holds the present world record: 2:51:01—making her the oldest person ever to qualify for the Olympic trials in track and field.

At 5 feet 1 inch, 102 pounds, Toshiko has a wonderfully athletic body and spirit. "I look at running more as requiring mental ability and guts rather than physical strength. And as I grow older, I feel more than ever we should look at the sport on a long-term basis, to keep our state of health the first priority."

60s Adrienne Salmini of Yonkers, New York, is 67 years old, and all 5 feet 6 inches and 125 pounds of her is filled with a love for life and sport. She took up running at age 62 and does 4 to 6 miles a day, in addition to ballroom and Hawaiian dancing, painting, sewing, and making quilts. She has run 185 races and won 180 trophies. Although she has always been active and remembers enjoying running up and down during high school field hockey, she never dreamed she'd start running until her sons gave her a pair of running shoes and a warm-up suit and urged her to get going. She is fit in both body and spirit, and each day when she runs, she says a prayer of thanks for her strength.

70s Margaret Lopez was sorry to miss the 1983 New York City Marathon, in which she had participated the previous two years and run her best time of 5:04. She was busy, however, biking 730 miles down the California coast.

Margaret began running six years ago and now, with the coaching help of her son, logs 35 to 40 miles a week, including one track workout a week of quarter and half miles. Her advice to anyone is to "just get out and run. It's the most wonderful thing that ever happened to me." At 5 feet 5¼ inches and 125 pounds ("and all muscle," she adds proudly), Margaret has a new job since she retired from teaching. She sells fish, and lifts 20- to 40-pound bunches of them all day long.

80s Ruth Rothfarb is under 5 feet tall, and all 100 pounds of her belong to the oldest woman ever to complete a marathon—and she's done it several times. Ruth ran a remarkable 5:37:28 in the New York City Marathon at age 80, and her time was over one hour faster than the man in her age category!

She took up running at age 72 after watching her son and grandson compete in a race, and began to run 10 miles a day. Ruth, who was never particularly athletic, says, "I love running; I've found my niche. When I hear about people my age getting lonesome and depressed, that's not for me. I would highly recommend running for people of my age who are in good health."

90s Gwen Clark used to sit in Central Park and watch the runners, until one day she thought she'd follow them "to see where they were going." She was 86 years old when she began to race walk. Today at 92 she walks the 7-mile loop of the park from her apartment and back in 2½ hours. For those 2½ hours every morning, she's the talk of Central Park. Runners and spectators alike greet her, and get a needed jolt of inspiration. Her daily exercise doesn't end in the park however. At night she does a half hour of upper-body and leg exercises.

A retired nurse originally from New Zealand, Gwen says, "I was ashamed of the shape I let myself get in. Now my posture has improved and I feel stronger. I'm feeling what the muscles can do. Fitness is a tour of exploration of the body." Now that older people are doing more exercise, Gwen's advice for those who want to get into a sport is, "Go into it easily, and have a good time with it."

There are no promises of a magic revival by running in the later years. But in his mid-60s George Sheehan knows the secret of running with the years. "I see age as an asset. Not a day passes when I don't learn more about my craft. Perhaps I don't learn enough to compensate entirely for the loss of strength and endurance that occurs inexorably each year—but enough so that everything except the stopwatch tells me I am now running better than I ever have."

You can always run, no matter how old you are. It's a good way to challenge yourself, and the society that claims life grows limited with the years. As Sheehan rightly concludes, "People may retire you, but life never does."

9

Interviews with Top Women Runners

JOAN BENOIT

TEMPORARILY LEAVING THE woods of her native Maine, Joan Benoit emerges to run a race. When she does she leaves her carefully guarded interests: her friends, her own house she is busy remodeling, stamp collecting, knitting, canning preserves, lobster trapping and cooking—and, regrettably, her privacy.

There's no diplomatic way to put it: Joan Benoit hates the publicity, the interviews, and attention her accomplishments have brought her, probably more than any other elite runner. She is the most introverted of an already introverted species—the distance runner.

She is exactly what *Sports Illustrated* has called her: "The Marathon's Maine Woman." She is a composite of the world's fastest woman marathoner and a 100 percent product of the state of Maine: the type of person who loves the outdoors and the simple life. "Joanie," as she is affectionately referred to by friends and admirers, cherishes her privacy.

She realized after her 1979 Boston Marathon win that there was an aspect of the victory she hadn't considered: the overwhelming attention it brought. Her quiet world was invaded, and it produced a trauma that would permanently affect her. Only years later would she say she had finally come to terms with the attention, although she still does not enjoy it. She swore after that Boston race and the endless phone calls, requests, and surprise visits: "Never again am I going to put myself in this situation." Now, to keep the pressure off and the media away, she'll almost never commit herself to a race in advance. Sometimes she'll just show up on the starting line with no advance warning at all. Four years after her first Boston win, with a string of victories, American records, and the world marathon record to her credit, she still fights to make peace with the attention it brings her. In fact, the fame that resulted from her world record–shattering marathon caused her to move from the more public community of Boston to the seclusion of Maine.

More than just a world record in the 1983 Boston Marathon, it was by how much she cut that record that put Joan Benoit in a league by herself. Setting a pace that was called reckless and crazy ("The men kept saying, 'Lady, watch it'"), she sped through intermediate points in record time, passing elite men runners on her way to a time of 2:22:43, a new record by a full 2 minutes 46 seconds. "A ridiculous time," said an obviously speechless race announcer of a feat nothing less than astounding. Jack Welch wrote in *Track and Field News* that her accomplishment had added "if not another dimension, then certainly another plateau towards ultimate athletic achievement for women. She is alone."

Those who take a surface look say how unlike a typical elite distance runner Joan Benoit looks. They're surprised at what her 5-foot 3-inch, 103-pound body can do, stunned by the athletic daring of someone with a pixie haircut and such soft, round blue eyes. But those in the know talk about her tremendous efficiency as a runner, her fluid stride and rapid leg turnover. She's got the equipment; her maximum oxygen uptake (VO_2 max)* of 79 is the highest for any woman runner tested. Above all, coaches, journalists, and peers agree—her concentration and competitive drive are unparalleled in the running world. These are the qualities that separate the good from the best, and Joan Benoit has them.

Even in her childhood her love of victory was evident. Her father remembers her winning her first ski race when she was only in the third grade. "You could see the exhilaration in her face," he says. Her Athletics West coach Bob Sevene says she's the most tenacious athlete he's ever worked with. Joan herself claims she doesn't know why she's so competitive; her parents didn't instill it in her, nor her brothers. "Sometimes they say it's survival of the fittest," she admits. "As a child, I wanted one of the three baseball gloves. There were four of us, and only three gloves."

Born the third child and the only girl of four, tomboy Joan started out as a ski racer, sprinter, long jumper, and basketball player. After a skiing accident she began distance running for rehabilitation. She quickly achieved success. Yet in high school she remembers "practicing on my

*Maximum oxygen uptake (VO_2 max) is the maximum amount of oxygen that can be consumed, transported, and utilized by the body.

own during the weekends and summer months and being embarrassed to be seen on the roads."

She won her first race, a cross-country event, her junior year in high school, and was the state mile champion by her senior year. She attended Bowdoin College, and as there was no women's running team, she ran for the New England women's team Liberty AC. She competed to date in the Olympic trials 1500 meters in 1976, and laid the foundation for her future road racing success with her first of five wins to date in the prestigious Falmouth road race.

One of a group of top women runners in the 1970s including stand-outs Julie Shea and Margaret Groos, Joan has emerged as the best. Running journalist Toni Reavis, who has documented her career, believes it is due to her strong athletic background and steady personality. "She's a Maine-type person," he says, referring to her calm and patient nature, which coupled with her phenomenal determination has created her blend of success.

She has learned a lot in her 27 years, especially from those women distance runners who have made it and subsequently crumbled. "You can't keep pushing and pushing, testing and testing," she says from her own experience and observing others. "Personal best times don't come overnight, and motivations aren't a dime a dozen." She knows that racing too often or from the lure of the limelight won't produce consistent results. When Joan goes to the starting line, she says she has to be hungry—eager and raring to go. She knows that in more ways than one, timing is everything.

The lessons haven't come without their price. She found that out five years ago when she raced 10 kilometers and the next day intended to run only a part of the marathon as a training run, but felt good and ran the entire 26.2 miles, all in 2:50. Less than a week later, she ran a 2-mile and 800 meter races on the track, and that solidified the damage. For days even walking was painful. She had developed Achilles tendon problems that would eventually require surgery. But after the operations on both Achilles in 1980, and the scars (her heels look like a relief map), and the days she pumped a stationary bike with casts on her feet with characteristic determination—Joan Benoit emerged a winner, just as she did way back in the third grade after her first ski race.

For an athlete, her personality seems enigmatic: the shyness mixed with such competitive drive. Yet the way she puts it, it's all black and white. "Running is a big part of my life, but not the only part," she concludes. "There's really no rhyme or reason to my training," she says, and one would believe she runs without much focus or plan. Yet attacking the hills while training in Maine, she is nothing less than ferocious, determined—undoubtedly with her eye on the marathon Olympic gold medal. She says she runs best with a lot on her mind, when she's angry, under pressure, or busy—like now, fixing her new house.

She is, above all, still that shy, private girl. She has her friends, and a longtime boyfriend, whom she has announced she is to marry in August in 1984—but none of them are part of the running scene. Her life is strictly divided between public and private. However, she is undoubtedly just as obsessed with her running as most people, but maybe with more reason. She's a world record holder. When forced to take off she gets the running addict's itch. "I miss it; I'm less productive, less happy," she says, speaking in short, nervous sentences.

As for her competitive career, she feels, "My biggest concern is to see self-improvement." When her racing days are over, she will probably continue to run. After all, she does it because she "just likes to run." Beyond the Olympics, the next three years will somehow be occupied with her promotions commitment for Dole Pineapple, sponsors of the first women's Olympic marathon trials.

No matter how many accolades she acquires from her success in the running world, Joan Benoit is still that Maine woman at heart. "There's nothing more inviting than having a place to call home," she says with her basic love of being rooted, and in a rare moment of revelation she adds, "Someday I'd like to have a family."

JULIE BROWN

Runner's World magazine has called Julie Brown "the female equivalent of Bill Rodgers and Steve Scott combined"—a composite of the best of both marathoner and miler. In fact, her talent over 26.2 miles is equaled only by her success at the shorter distances. Her marathon time of 2:26:24 currently ranks her fourth in the world, and with her successive and steady improvement, she's moving up. She says the 2:26 effort, which she ran unchallenged to win the 1983 Avon International Marathon title by a full mile, was remarkably easy. Julie knows she can go faster, and she knows what drives her: the gold. "My whole energy is geared for the 1984 Olympics." She has no qualms about admitting how much she wants that medal. "To be the best at something, it has to be an obsession," she concludes.

Over the years 28-year-old Julie Brown has been America's most successful and versatile runner. She is a Pan American Games medalist in the 800, 1500, and 3,000 meters, an Olympian at 1500 meters, and the 1975 World Cross Country champion—a prestigious title that remains her most satisfying. In her first marathon she set an American record of 2:36:23, and she has never looked back, cutting two to five minutes off her personal best times in her last three completed marathons.

The middle child of five, Julie grew up in Montana, where the severe winters forced her to train in the halls of her high school, and the summers were so hot that she "didn't even think about running." At 18 she made the United States junior team and competed in Russia, West Germany, and Poland.

Despite her early accomplishments, Julie says she was not given just recognition. "Women in athletics weren't taken seriously. The popular girl in high school was a majorette or a cheerleader. But I was more into doing things for myself than cheering for someone else. It was frustrating because I was the state champion, and had I been a guy, I would have been recognized in my school. Since I was a woman they didn't pay much attention."

Julie did not consider herself a tomboy. Like many top women runners, what she did was who she was, not just a peripheral part of her identity or a form of role rebellion. And as with almost all top runners, her competitive drive has always been enormous, and her quest for perfection unending. "I don't like to lose," she says, "at anything." Even cutting five minutes off her time in the 1982 New York City Marathon was ultimately unsatisfying because she came in second in the race. "I don't enjoy my improvement as much as I should because I always expect more from myself," she admits, and although it was no less than Grete Waitz she was chasing, she says, "I felt like I should have won that race."

Most people are inherently competitive, philosophizes Julie, and she acknowledges that everyone wants recognition. Despite the fact that her family was not athletic, it was through sports that as the middle child she sought that recognition. Sports were her natural vehicle. "I was lucky to know at a young age that I had an ability for endurance sports. It's a natural physical ability I was born with." At 5 feet 6 inches and 107 pounds, Julie has an oxygen uptake of 76 and a scant body fat level of 6 percent— remarkable statistics even for an elite male runner—and together with her 83 percent slow twitch muscle fibers,* she is an ideal combination of the necessary physical attributes for a superior distance runner.

Julie runs between 100 and 110 miles a week, but feels numbers have little meaning as mileage needs vary greatly with the individual. She be-

---

*Muscles consist of fast and slow twitch fibers; the fast twitch fibers are utilized for explosive speed, and the slow twitch for endurance. Everyone possesses some combination of the two.

lieves slow mileage only puts stress on the body, so she alleviates that problem by running no slower than a 6- to 6:10-minute pace per mile. Two to three times a week she does harder workouts, and each of her two-a-day runs are sandwiched between stretching exercises. She presently lives in Eugene, Oregon—home of many top runners—where she is coached by the University of Oregon's Bill Dellinger, coach of many world-class competitors, including Alberto Salazar. She believes that 10,000 meters is probably her best distance, but doesn't put a lot of effort into it since it's not an Olympic event.

Over the years Julie has learned to improve what she says is her greatest weakness: impatience. "I want things to happen now, but as I get older I realize you can't get to the top without climbing." And she knows what it takes to climb high. "What you put into something is what you get out. If you lack ability but you put in the effort, you can still have success. A lot of it is your own determination."

Julie Brown understands that attitude and mental outlook are just as important to her success as physical conditioning. Before big races, she practices visualization—vividly picturing herself achieving her goal. She works hard at painting a mental picture of success. "Mental training is a lot like physical training; you have to keep up with it to get anything," she points out.

From the first day she stepped on a starting line, Julie has had to learn to deal with the anxiety of racing. "I still have the nerves. I think if you lose that you should retire, but it's not from fear, like I had before. It's from anticipation and excitement. And I still have the competitiveness, because if I lose that, it's a sign it's probably over for me."

After all the dreams for the Olympic marathon, what's left to dream when it's over? "Sure there will be a letdown," she realizes. "Whatever happens, so much of your time and energy is invested for two and a half hours, and then it's over, but that's true in any aspect of life. Once you set a goal and attempt it, it's over. You have to move on. If I can win the gold, I won't have the need to compete anymore."

Whether her goals will always involve running, Julie doesn't know. She'd someday like to pursue her other interests like skiing, and perhaps the medical career she considered when she got her degree in biology. But for now her sights are set on one target. "Once I set a goal, I'm narrow-minded. I have to get it." If the gold doesn't hang from her neck in 1984, it is certain she has the ability, and the drive, to see it sparkle in 1988.

WOMEN'S RUNNING HISTORY

1896   Melpomene, having been denied entry to the first Olympic marathon because she is a woman, unofficially runs the race in 4:30.

Married Ladies' Foot Race. Competitors dressed in their Sunday finest hold up their skirts at the starting line on the Santa Monica Pier, California, 1916. (Courtesy of Avon Products, Inc., and photo historian Ernest Marquez)

1918   Marie Ledru runs the French Marathon and finishes 38th.

1924   Requests for women's track events in the Olympics are denied by the International Amateur Athletic Federation (IAAF).

1926   Violet Piercy of Great Britain runs a marathon in 3:40:22.

1928   Three women's track events are added to the Olympic program. The 800-meter run is among them, but it is stricken from future games when horrified officials witness the collapse of two untrained competitors at the finish. Not until 1960 is the event reinstated.

Fanny Blankers-Koen winning the 200 meters in the 1948 Olympics. (AP/Wide World Photos)

1948   An early superstar, Fanny Blankers-Koen of the Netherlands wins Olympic gold medals in all four women's track events at the London Games. Her accomplishments are considered particularly remarkable because she is 30 years old (the oldest competitor in the '48 Olympics) and the mother of two young sons.

THE SIXTIES—Determination, commitment, and perseverance mark a decade of continuing political and social obstacles in women's running.

1960   The 800-meter event is reinstated and remains the longest women's.Olympic track event until the 1972 Games, when the 1500 meters is added.

1964   Dale Greig of Great Britain runs a 3:27 marathon, and Mildred Simpson of New Zealand clocks a 3:19. Dr. Ernst van Aaken of West Germany begins to speak out in support of women's long-distance running, but attitudes, particularly in the United States, are slow to change.

1966   Roberta Gibb unofficially completes the Boston Marathon in 3:20, becoming the first woman ever to run this prestigious event.

1967   Kathrine Switzer, drawing publicity to the exclusion of women competitors, enters the Boston Marathon as K.V. Switzer and finishes the race despite attempts by angry officials to throw her off the course. The same year Anni Pede Erdkamp of West Germany sets a new women's world marathon mark of 3:07:26.

1968   Under increased pressure from the lobbying efforts of accomplished women runners, the AAU (the governing body for running in the United States) finally sanctions women's races up to 5 and then to 10 miles.

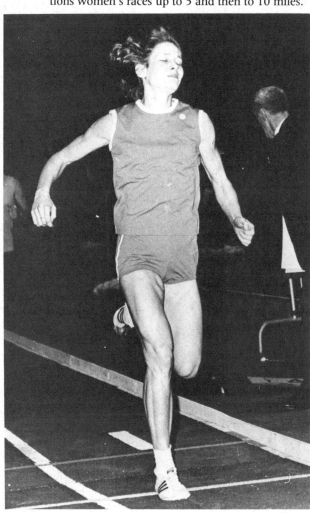

Doris Brown Heritage, 5-time National and 5-time World Cross Country Champion from 1967 to 1971. (Courtesy of **New York Running News)**

THE SEVENTIES—Milestone victories occur in a decade of shattered records and tremendous growth in participation.

1971   Beth Bonner clocks 2:55:22 in the New York City Marathon, becoming the first American woman to break the 3-hour barrier.

1972   The AAU approves women's official participation in the marathon and Nina Kuscsik, pioneer advocate of women's distance running, becomes the first official female winner of the Boston Marathon.

Seventy-eight women compete in the first women's-only 10-kilometer road race, paving the way for what would become, ten years later, the most prestigious women's long distance road race in the world, the Mini Marathon.

1973   West Germany holds the first National Women's Marathon Championship in October. Five months later the United States follows suit in San Mateo, California, where forty-four of the fifty-seven starters finish the race. The winning time is 2:55:17.

1975   The first Colgate Women's Games are held in New York City with 5,000 young women competing. The meet is started by Fred Thompson, coach of the highly successful women's team: the Atoms Track Club. By 1983 the games draw 22,000, making it the world's largest sporting event for women.

1978   Grete Waitz of Norway, running in her first marathon in New York, stuns the world with a 2:32:30 world record. She goes on to a repeat performance in 1979 (2:27:33, the first woman under 2:30) and again in 1980 (2:25:42). In 3 years the women's world marathon record is lowered by almost 10 minutes.

The first Avon all-women's marathon is held in Atlanta.

In a discussion of the widespread distribution of payment in the form of under-the-table money, top coach Bill Squires wrote that in 1978, "The only thing a woman runner could expect to receive under the table when competing in a track meet was a game of footsie."

The first Avon all-women's marathon in Atlanta, 1978. The number of participants in this race increased 600 percent by 1983. (Janeart, Ltd./Courtesy of Avon Products, Inc.)

1979   Avon Products creates the first International Running Circuit for women, offering a program of races of varying distances for all levels of competition. Within 3 years the Avon Circuit has grown to fifty races in nineteen countries.

The National Running Data Center in Tucson, Arizona, estimates that there are more than 95,000 female performances in road races from 5km to the marathon in the United States during 1979. There are more than 8,000 marathon performances by women around the world. In the New York City Marathon alone, the number of female competitors leaps from 88 in 1976 to 1,780 in 1979.

THE EIGHTIES—A new era is launched by the worldwide focus on women athletes, but experts caution we have only just begun.

1980   Grete Waitz, leading more than 5,000 women in the L'eggs Mini Marathon, sets a women's world 10,000-meter record of 30:59.8.

Mary Decker begins her 2-year assault on women's world track records by thrilling a standing crowd of 18,000 at the Millrose Games with a world indoor 1500-meter record (4:00:8).

1981   For the 4th consecutive year a new women's world marathon record is set at the New York City Marathon. Allison Roe of New Zealand lowers the mark to 2:25:29, a time that would have won a gold medal at every Olympic Games marathon until 1952.

The starting line of the 1981 New York City Marathon in which more than 2,500 women ran. Allison Roe is on the far right, wearing gloves. Leg pains forced Grete Waitz (#F1) to drop out of the race at 15 miles. (Leo Kulinski, Jr.)

1982   The Soviet Union holds its first all-women's marathon, won by Arina Zinurova in 2:42:46, a national record.

Mary Decker breaks seven women's world and/or American records at distances ranging from 800 to 10,000 meters. She becomes the first woman to win the coveted Jesse Owens Award, bestowed annually to the United States' premier track and field competitor.

The International Olympic Committee grants final approval for the addition of a women's marathon and a 3,000-meter event to be held for the first time at the 1984 Olympic Games in Los Angeles. But the battle for the 5,000 and 10,000 meters rages on. Activists, such as former marathon world record holder Jacqueline Hansen, have now become prominent in the political arena of women's running.

Grete Waitz, queen of the roads, winning her 4th consecutive L'eggs Mini Marathon in 1982. (Ken Levinson)

1983   Joan Benoit shatters the women's world marathon mark with her time of 2:22:43. In the same Boston Marathon race, sixty women break 3 hours; 552 of the 652 female starters finish in under 4 hours, including two who are over 60 years of age. The average time for women is 3:20:58.

More than 250 women qualify for the first women's Olympic marathon trials held in May of 1984 in Olympia, Washington. They have equaled or bettered the 2:51:16 qualifying time.

Joan Benoit savors victory after her world record Boston Marathon run in 1983. (Duomo/Courtesy of Nike, Inc.)

WORLD RECORD PROGRESSION IN THE MARATHON

3:19:33	Mildred Simpson (New Zealand) 1964
3:15:22	Maureen Wilton (Canada) 1967
3:07:26	Anni Erdkamp (West Germany) 1967
3:02:53	Carolyn Walker (United States) 1970
3:01:42	Beth Bonner (United States) 1971
2:55:22	Beth Bonner (United States) 1971
2:49:40	Cheryl Bridges (United States) 1971
2:46:36	Miki Gorman (United States) 1973
2:46:24	Chantal Langlace (France) 1974
2:43:54	Jacqueline Hansen (United States) 1974
2:42:24	Liane Winter (West Germany) 1975
2:40:16	Christa Vahlensieck (West Germany) 1975
2:38:19	Jacqueline Hansen (United States) 1975
2:35:16	Chantal Langlace (France) 1977
2:34:48	Christa Vahlensieck (West Germany) 1977
2:32:30	Grete Waitz (Norway) 1978
2:27:33	Grete Waitz (Norway) 1979
2:25:42	Grete Waitz (Norway) 1980
2:25:29	Allison Roe (New Zealand) 1981
2:22:43	Joan Benoit (United States) 1983

In 5 days, Mary Decker lowers two American records—1500 meters to 3:57:12, and 800 meters to 1:57:60. She becomes a double gold medalist in the 1500 and 3,000 meters in the World Championships in Helsinki.

With talent and guts, Mary Decker wins the 1500 meters at the World Championships in Helsinki, as Soviet Zamira Zaitseva falls across the line for second. (AP/Wide World Photos)

Mary Decker and Grete Waitz are two of over fifty elite women runners who file a sex discrimination suit because of the exclusion of the 5,000 and 10,000 meters in the 1984 Olympic Games.

6,222 women runners join together to race in the 12th L'eggs Mini Marathon, whose slogan is, "Who says women can't run the world?"

7,000 women compete in the Bonne Bell 10-Kilometer Finals in Boston.

8,944 women enter the Evening Press/Brooks 10-Kilometer Mini Marathon in Dublin, Ireland, the largest all-women's field ever assembled for any race.

936 women from thirty countries compete in the Sixth Annual Avon International Marathon in Los Angeles. The race is broadcast live on national television and determines the U.S. Women's National Marathon Team for the first World Championships in Helsinki, Finland.

"No one could watch a finish like we had today and still say that women's races aren't exciting," said Britain's Wendy Sly (left) after her dramatic victory over America's Betty Springs, in the inaugural IAAF Women's 10-Kilometer Road Championships in December 1983. (Janeart, Ltd./Courtesy of Avon Products, Inc.)

"The Feeling." (Courtesy of **New York Running News***)*

Grete Waitz and Anne Audain embrace after Audain's victory in the 1983 L'eggs Mini Marathon. Redefinition of the competitive ethic may be one of the most meaningful results of the women's running movement. (Nancy Coplon)

Many experts agree that in most cases women can run safely through pregnancy. This woman gave birth four days after this photo was taken. (Tim Niederman/Courtesy of New York Running News)

Ninety-two-year-old Gwen Clark racewalks 7 miles daily. (Ken Levinson)

An early lesson in fun and fitness. (Ken Levinson)

MARY DECKER

800 meters, 1:57:60; 1500 meters, 3:57:12; the mile, 4:18:08; 3,000 meters, 8:29:71; 5,000 meters, 15:08:26; 10,000 meters 31:35.3—they're all American records, and the 5,000 is a world record. Yet the harsh logic of the numbers—distance, minutes, seconds—seems to belie the woman they belong to, and what she does. More than times and numbers express, it's how Mary Decker makes them happen—her style, her aura. More than the best female middle distance runner in America, and vying to be undisputably the best in the world, she is an artist: a study of beautiful motion coming alive on the run, possessed of her sport, and living for it above all else. "I want to give 100 percent of myself to my sport," she says. And that she does.

She's had the gift since the first time she ran. Even then, as an 11-year-old girl from Huntington Beach, California, who won the first race she ever ran, it was there. Never mind that she went to the event because she was bored and happened to read a notice about a cross-country race, and never mind that she didn't even know what cross-country was. She had always been and still is long legs and arms, down to the hands and fingers—with no place to go but forward, and no way to do it but fast. The cliché cries out to be quoted: born to run. As her coach Dick Brown says, Mary is "just plain gifted."

The gift has taken her far, but the way has not always been so easy. In fact, she's run into disaster at almost the same speed she's reached the finish line of a race. And it's been painful. As a child, she used her new-found running talent as an escape from the pain of her parents' divorce. Her daily training and weekly racing rewarded her, and her career bloomed. By age 14 she had run her first world record, for the 1,000 meters; by 16, she had run in more countries than most people see in a lifetime: at least ten of them, including the U.S.S.R., Poland, Japan, and Senegal. By then she had set three world records and captured a place in the hearts of the American people by beating a Russian in a U.S.A.-U.S.S.R. track meet.

Mary Decker, still in braces and pigtails, graced the cover of magazines—a child athlete no less a star than Shirley Temple. Yet despite her success at a tender age, she was pushing too hard. Little Mary Decker once ran a marathon (an outstanding 3:01 on no experience), the 440, the 880, the mile, and the 2-mile—all in just seven days. Doctors claimed it was the stress of that week that necessitated her emergency appendectomy the following day. Today Mary Decker says that despite it all she is not sorry she ran so hard so soon. "I just love to run. I always have. Nobody has ever forced me. The only time I feel bad is when I can't go out and run." If Mary Decker had not been forced over the years to learn her body's limits, she would probably still run endlessly, intensely. For her, running is all.

Today, however, at 25 years old, she has learned her limit, and she's got the scars to prove it. By 1974, it was stress fractures, and by 1976 she could hardly walk due to crippling leg pains. She had already spent a summer in casts on both feet when she was 13, and her troubles were just beginning. By 16, she was a self-acknowledged has-been, retired from running by a body riddled with injury. But Mary Decker never quit. Her lower leg pains were so intense when she tried to run that she began a search for relief that would last three years and take her from doctor to doctor, treatment to treatment: in casts, out of casts, X-rays, drugs—some so strong they made her legs swell and her hair fall out.

Finally, as if waking up from a nightmare, she found a solution. It was discovered that her leg pains were due to a rare condition called compartment syndrome, which results in the painful expansion of the sheaths surrounding the calf muscles. The sheaths could not accommodate her developed calf muscles, which began to expand with blood when she ran. In two operations the sheaths were slit, and in healing they filled with scar tissue, making them able to accommodate the expanded muscles.

Injuries did not end there, however. More surgery for Achilles tendinitis sidelined her for sixteen months in 1980, and subsequently her brilliant career has still been continually marred by aches and pains, muscle pulls, and layoffs. "Mary's legs are a mass of scar tissue and knots," says her Athletics West masseur. Of all the top runners he works with, he must spend the most time with Mary, kneading and pounding to keep her brilliant career uninterrupted.

Since Mary began working with Athletics West coach and physiologist Dick Brown, her injuries finally seem under control. She has begun to channel her passion for running by limiting her intense training. In the summer of 1983, she demonstrated worldwide superiority in winning two gold medals in the 1500 and 3,000 meters in the World Championships in Helsinki, giving the powerful Russian women a dose of defeat they would not soon forget.

Too young for the 1972 Olympics, disabled by injury for the 1976 Games, and a victim of the boycott of the 1980 competition, Mary Decker's passion is clear: the 1984 Olympic Games in Los Angeles. As this book goes to press, she has spent the months leading up to the event training in the seclusion in her adopted home of Eugene, Oregon, continuing with the program that has succeeded in keeping her injury-free. She runs no more than 60 quality miles a week, often accompanied by male running escorts to make sure she doesn't overdo it. "I don't have to be pushed," she acknowledges. "I have to be held back."

Mary Decker continues to break all the rules, as well as the records. Unlike the young child running stars who tire of the activity or burn out, she has had a continually fueled enthusiasm for running in her 14-year-long career. Her perseverance is a result of her adversity. She is determined, she says, "because of all I've been through. Every injury, every operation, has taken its toll, physically, mentally, and emotionally. But each time I've been hurt, it's just made me more determined to come back again."

Mary Decker is more than an athlete; she is a gifted performer. "I honestly think of running as an art form," she says. "Watching a great race is like looking at a pretty picture." By her own admission that is just what she strives to create. Her shiny red track briefs cling to her 5-foot 6-inch, 107-pound perfect body, a body that *Vanity Fair* magazine saw fit to feature in an artistic swimsuit spread. She is always sure to primp before a race, wearing sufficient makeup and jewelry for any performer, even one whose stage is a 400-meter track. Her feminine athlete image seems to work. The audience loves her, and she loves them—and the cheering. Says Mary with the polish of a professional actor, "I try to get a sense of the crowd." And she does, bringing them to their feet in wild adulation. When she stepped to the line for the indoor mile in the Millrose Games in 1981, the capacity crowd fell in love with her. "Mary, Mary, Mary," they shouted to the rhythm of her stride, and as they did, she said, they drove her to a world record.

Mary Decker's entire life has been running; she has known little else. Except for three years at the University of Colorado as a physical education major, where she also immersed herself in running, her only other brief employment besides her sport has been selling shoes in a running store. Today, from obvious necessity, she runs full-time, making a sizable six-figure per year income from training allowances, race awards money, and endorsements. In addition to her stipend, her medical and training needs are taken care of by the elite Nike-sponsored team Athletics West, of which she was the first woman member.

Mary Decker's definition of herself is her career. Competitive urge is never a problem to summon—it is always there. A foot on the track is enough to stoke her competitive fire. "I am a competitive person," she admits. "I get myself into that frame of mind when I race."

Mary Decker goes after what she wants almost ruthlessly. Her focus is clear, and she allows no one to stand in her way. In the 1983 Millrose

Games, onlookers gasped in shock as she pushed a slower runner she had lapped out of her way. After the demise of her twenty-two-month marriage to marathoner Ron Tabb, he said, "I wanted to feel that I was the most important thing in her life. But to Mary, her career is her life."

Even of those possessed with greatness, we often expect the values we hold for everyone. We respect Grete Waitz when she says her running is not everything in life, and we are relieved. Not so with Mary Decker. She makes her motives and her goals clear. "You can be the best friends with someone off the track," she says, "but in the race, only one person can win."

Perhaps, however, we should judge differently this woman who has what it takes to achieve greatness, because despite the gold earrings and makeup, and the fluid stride with its unbelievable perfection, those long lines of tiny white scars that decorate Mary Decker's shins say the most about what she's gone through to get where she is. Perhaps we should remember our own dreams, and realize how few of us can dream of Olympic gold, or feel that it has eluded us three times, for thirteen years. Whatever the stakes, Mary Decker is betting that it won't elude her again.

NINA KUSCSIK

No one has done more for women's distance running and achieved such personal running success as Nina Kuscsik. In fact, she doesn't mind the fact that she's commonly referred to as a pioneer of women's running, although she's reluctant to call her motives altruistic. "When pioneers went out West they didn't think they were going to pave the way for those coming after them," she says. "They were explorers; they were doing it for themselves."

Yet whatever her initial motive when she began, by virtue of her political involvement as well as her running accomplishments, Nina has helped pave the way for those women who run today, and made what was once a rocky road smooth. "The issues seemed to me to be so clear," she says of the fight for equality in women's distance running she began over a decade ago. "For me not to do something would have been so much more out of character than to take action."

Since shortly after she began her running career fifteen years ago, Nina has been active in lobbying for legislation that has aided in the acceptance and development of women's distance running. Working with the AAU, now the TAC (The Athletics Congress), the governing body for the sport, Nina has been as effective behind the scenes as she was in her well-known public protest, a sit-down strike by the women in the 1972 New York City Marathon demanding equality with the men. It was about this time that Nina realized, "There were other women adults who still loved sport, and were serious about it."

Her own love of sport resulted in the following accomplishments: the first official winner of the Boston Marathon in 1972; New York City Marathon winner in 1972 and 1973; one of the first two American women to break three hours for the marathon with her 2:56:04 in New York in 1971; and an American women's record for 50 miles in 1977.

Nina was no newcomer to athletics. As an adult she loved sports, as she had while a young girl. As a teenager in her native Brooklyn, Nina had been an all-around athlete—a champion roller skater, speed skater, figure skater, and bicyclist.

Nina started running in the summer of 1967, and ran her first race in Boston in 1969 on 30 miles of training a week. A marathon is a long way to run for the first race, but she says, "That was the only race I knew of." She immediately felt the lure of the sport. "What has always excited me about races is that the improvement is so measurable. There's a starting line, a finish line, and a stopwatch. I love the challenge, and to see the improvement."

Nina joined a running club after her initial success, but as those were the days when running ended with childhood, she found she was twice the age of the oldest member. Although she has never technically had a coach, she thought about getting one to maximize her chances of qualifying for the first women's Olympic marathon trials. She claims she has no regrets that all the glitter and the perks weren't there for a woman runner in the early days, but she does say, "Once in a while I wonder how much more developed I would have become if running had been there for me when I was younger."

Nina has learned a lot over the years about the joys and conflicts of being a woman athlete. "I used to stand on a starting line and ask myself how I could care so much about one thing. Did it mean I didn't care about other things? 'What's more important,' I would ask, 'This race or. . . .' I looked around and wondered how so many people could make this choice. I didn't realize at the time that you didn't have to choose. Now I know you can care about a lot of things; it's just that everything has its time." If it weren't running that occupied her time and energy, dividing her attention from those she felt wanted or needed it, she says it probably would have been something else. "You can't always be totally available for everybody else." This was a big realization for a divorced woman raising three children. Nina had to learn to do it all.

The years have also taught her other valuable lessons one can learn only from experience. "I don't know if it's from getting older, or experience, but I've learned your body is your leader; you are not your body's leader. You can show it the pathways, but your body is only going to go when it's ready."

Nina is presently the chairman of the Women's Long Distance Committee and is on the board of directors of TAC and the New York Road Runners Club. For her invaluable service, she has received the TAC president's award, the New York Road Runners Club service award, and been voted into the Road Runners Club of America Hall of Fame. A major force behind the acceptance of the first women's Olympic marathon in 1984, Nina also supports the legal suit calling for the women's 5,000 meters and 10,000 meters to be put in the Games. "Look at these women who have to make choices that the men don't have to make," she argues, referring to the gap in Olympic distances between the 3,000 meters, slightly under 2 miles, and the 26.2-mile marathon.

For her athletic accomplishments, and her work in women's running, Nina has made personal sacrifices, and is not without conflicts. "I still have that feeling I have not been totally available for my children," she laments. Yet surely her two grown sons and daughter are as proud of the respect she commands as she is. In a recent election for board members of the New York Road Runners Club, out of a maximum possible vote of 25 percent of the 23,000 membership, Nina got 24.2 percent. Considering that the nearest among the incumbent competitors gained only 17.5 percent, Nina's result is even more outstanding. Everybody respects Nina Kuscsik, and with good reason.

MARCY SCHWAM

Marcy Schwam has been in perpetual motion all 31 years of her life. In high school she played every possible sport, and was a competitive tennis player throughout college, achieving a measure of success in tournament play. But no matter what she played in her native White Plains, New York, or what she did, she did it on the run.

Marcy started to run at age 15 as conditioning for tennis, and ended up running everywhere—to and from the train station, to and from the office, to and from the tennis courts. Eventually she even gave up using her car, and ran.

It's no wonder that today Marcy Schwam is the best female ultradistance runner in the world. She holds the world record for 50 miles (5:59:25); the world track records for 50 miles, 100 kilometers, and 100 miles—all set in a 24-hour race in November of 1981; and the American road record for 100 kilometers (8:47:28). Early in her career she established herself as both a record breaker and a ground breaker, becoming the first woman to complete the 72-mile run around Lake Tahoe, California, in September of 1978.

Marcy's accomplishments not only are significant for their number and scope, but they place her higher in overall standings among both men and women than in any other running events. Her 50-mile world record, in which she came in third overall among 100 men, is matched by a second place overall in a six-day race, and tenth overall in her first showing in the Lake Tahoe run.

Obviously there are not many who can physically or mentally withstand the rigors of ultra-distance running, but for Marcy it has been natural right from the beginning. She's got the requirements. "I always liked constant movement. And I enjoy training and running by myself." She discovered her proclivity for ultra running in 1977 when she went on a "marathon spree"—running 11 of the 26.2-mile races in a year, a marathon a month. She never got tired. In fact, she felt great. She then ran her first ultra, a 50-kilometer race, followed by a 40-miler, which she won. Success resulted in an increase in her training to 100 miles a week.

Her physical stamina is extraordinary: maintaining an average of 120 miles a week over the years with one to two speed sessions on the track and weight lifting—one is more than a little inclined to wonder how her body does it. "Luck," says Marcy most definitively. Luck and, she says, her intense lifelong athletic background, from which she has built physical strength and endurance. Marcy's range is unsurpassed by any woman ultra runner. Her 10-kilometer best (35:44) and marathon (2:48:17) are outstanding by any standards, not to mention that those are just warm-up distances for a woman who races from 100 miles to 6 days.

It's what it takes mentally, however, that's most intriguing about ultra running. Says Marcy of the sport, "It's nothing except you and your mind. Ultra running is more mental toughness than anything. You simply must overcome going through the discomfort." What makes Marcy so superior at her sport is her stable character and her complete inner confidence and strength. "I have a certain stability, a strong-mindedness." It's a stability she radiates, and her success is a result of her determination. Marcy Schwam has the necessary ingredient to excel: she believes in herself. "I accept success, and feel comfortable doing well," she says.

The running world has rewarded Marcy with numerous prestigious awards. For two consecutive years she has won the following: *Runner's World* magazine Paavo Nurmi Award; the New York Road Runners Club Outstanding Female Ultradistance runner, and *Ultra* magazine's top female runner. In so unique an occupation, requiring a will and endurance that few expect of a woman, one expects she has faced prejudice. "Never," she claims. "Only respect."

Her most difficult period was in 1983, when she was forced out of the New York Road Runners Club 100-Mile Invitational Run and the New York Six-Day Run. After settling into a comfortable 7-minute mile pace in the 100-miler, which would have broken the world record by 1 hour and 40 minutes, she was forced to drop out with pains in her injured foot. "My ego was shattered," she says. "I had put in nine months of serious training, and five or six months before the race I had tuned myself out to everything else." She was doing things she had never done before, including reading books on sports psychology. "To be so ready physically, and not be able to perform . . ." she laments. Marcy's goals are fueled by those experiences. After running the women's Olympic marathon trials, for which she qualified, she plans to set two world records in 1984: one in the 100-mile race, and the other in the Six-Day Run.

Marcy's future is aimed at taking her running career to the limit, "to see how far I can excel." And she's fighting to prove by her example that an ultra runner ought to be taken more seriously. "There's still the stigma attached to ultra runners that they aren't fast enough to succeed at other distances."

She will go far, as far as the heart and mind can take anyone as able and as dedicated as Marcy Schwam. "Doing well in racing comes from having a certain degree of inner freedom," she says with the wisdom of one who has looked long and hard within herself. "I've always had the attitude about things that I would survive, no matter what." More than just a survivor, Marcy Schwam is a winner.

GRETE WAITZ

In 1978, an unknown Norwegian crossed the finish line of the New York City Marathon with a world-record time of 2:32:30. From that moment on, life would never be the same for Grete Waitz. Her name would become linked to a new revolution in women's sports and distance running, and fame would follow her everywhere. But Grete's shy and unassuming behavior has remained the same. After three world records and a total of five victories in the New York City Marathon, her most memorable experience is her final day as an unknown. She says she will always remember the question that was asked after she crossed the line: "Who is number 1173?"

From that October Sunday in 1978, to the present height of her career at age 30, Grete has established herself as the greatest woman long-distance runner in history—the runner who made the world realize what a woman can do. It is widely acknowledged that her accomplishments led to the approval of the first women's Olympic marathon in 1984. She was the first woman to run under 2:30 in the marathon, destroying her own record by five minutes in only her second try at the distance, and has broken 2:30 five times, more than any other woman. She has won the prestigious World Cross Country Championships five times; won the New York City Marathon more times than any runner, man or woman; captured four titles in the L'eggs Mini Marathon, setting a world road record for 10 kilometers (30:59.8), and won the first-ever World Championships marathon in Helsinki in August, 1983.

None of this has changed the nature of the 30-year-old Grete, who despite her fame (a survey once revealed she is the second-most popular person in Norway, after the king!) feels unchanged. "I feel so very simple and normal myself; I want to be like everybody else, not special. I have never enjoyed fame." Far from displaying false modesty, Grete Waitz genuinely dislikes being in the public eye. When called upon to speak, she finds it hard to express her feelings. The nature of a Scandinavian is not like the open, revealing personality of an American, she says. Nonetheless, her feelings and opinions are there, and they reflect both wisdom, grace, and poise—qualities for which she is so respected.

Grete Anderson was born in Oslo, the youngest of three children and the only girl. "When my parents finally got a girl, they wanted me to be a nice little daughter. My first day of school I wore a pink dress, and pink ribbons in my hair, which was curled." Her girlhood, far from athletic, was centered on piano lessons, which much to her misery she was forced to endure for nine years. "I hated it. I kept asking my parents if I could stop, but they wouldn't let me. I'd have to practice at least forty-five minutes a day, and sometimes I was practicing and crying at the same time. I haven't touched a piano since I moved from my parents' house ten years ago."

When Grete began running at 13, her parents asked her why she was wasting so much time. They assumed it was another in the long line of her activities that kept her too busy—gymnastics, team handball, and now the track and field club. "You're never going to be a running star anyway," they told her. But when she won the junior title in the quarter and half mile at age 16, her parents sat up and took notice, and became more supportive of her running. When they saw that running was something special to her, and that she was good, they finally let her drop the piano lessons.

It was in the track and field club that young Grete met Jack Waitz, who would eventually become her husband and coach. Jack, who has always been supportive of his wife's career, admits, "I had always wanted to be a good runner myself, but I didn't have the talent. So what I didn't achieve for myself in sports, I feel I live through Grete's success." Grete credits Jack with much of that success, and says she could not get out and train hard all week without his support.

Up every morning at 5 a.m., Grete does a morning training run with Jack, which she follows with another training session in the afternoon. Her mileage, 70 to 90 per week, is never done slower than a 6-minute pace. As a former track runner who brings her speed training to the roads, long slow distance training makes little sense to Grete, who has achieved her success with hard interval-type training.* However, since she became a confirmed marathoner several years ago—a label she once spurned in favor of "track runner first, road runner second"—she has adapted her training to include one long run a week of at least 15 miles. This is quite an increase for a woman who ran her first marathon in world record time, having run no more than 10 miles at one time in her life! She proved then what every top road racer would soon learn: that it's quality, much more than quantity, that makes a good runner.

What puts Grete in a class by herself is not only her record-breaking achievements in distance running, but her maturity and longevity in a sport that can provide overwhelming success one day and disaster the next. The instantaneous media blitz and subsequent fame that accompany a New York City Marathon win have temporarily felled several great runners, including Alberto Salazar and Allison Roe. But with the exception of 1981, when Grete had to drop out of New York with shin splints, she has maintained her string of Marathon victories and withstood the subsequent attention with body and mind intact.

Her career has not been without its disappointments, however, made particularly difficult when judged by a fickle public that is quick to dismiss a sidelined champion as a has-been. In 1981, after Grete was forced to drop out of New York, she watched Allison Roe on the television set in her hotel room go on to win the race and take her world record. Determined to get her record back, she gave an all-out effort in the 1982 Boston Marathon,

---

*Interval training is running repeated set distances at relatively high intensity with recovery periods in between.

but pounding down the hills caused her to hobble off the course at 23 miles with crippling leg cramps. Some of the media, not known for their loyalty, pronounced her washed up. But hard-core fans knew otherwise, and Grete's patience and determination were rewarded by a victorious comeback.

Grete's values have changed over the years. "If I lost or did poorly in a race at twenty-four or twenty-five years old, that was the end of the world, but now I have a different attitude toward competition. I want to win, but if I don't, it's not the main thing. I want to enjoy running and be happy—that's more important to me than just winning races." The significance of this attitude is that she's managed to balance her life and her sport, a difficult task for anyone on top. And running isn't just a hobby or an avocation for Grete. Since she quit her teaching job in 1980, it has been her sole occupation.

If some runners seem obsessed or addicted, it would seem that could also be the case, if not the privilege, of the best runner in the world. But not so with Grete; she knows life's priorities. "Sometimes you have to put your feet on the ground and see running in the whole world perspective. What is running? Of course for me personally it's a big thing, but taking the whole world into account—running is just a little part of it."

Despite her undisputed title as "Queen of the Roads," she does not believe she is personally responsible for the acceptance of the first women's Olympic marathon in 1984. She knows, like many other women, that there's still a long way left to equality. In fact, she was one of the top women runners to file suit for the inclusion of the 5,000 and 10,000 meters for women in the Olympic Games.

Grete has been running competitively for twelve years, but it has only been in the last few years that injuries have plagued her. According to the doctors, she says, after all the years of intense running some places in her legs are very tight and the joints are wearing down. Will she compete indefinitely?

"I'll make up my mind after the 1984 Olympics, but I don't think so. In one way I look forward to retiring. To go out and train twice a day, all year round, is very hard."

No one deserves a rest more than Grete, but what lies beyond retirement is difficult to envision for the woman who has made running her life. "In another way I'm afraid of that day, because it's like a house in which the fourth wall just falls down. What will my life be like? I'm so used to this kind of life."

10

Women's Running Worldwide

A Look at the Sport in Some Other Countries

BRAZIL

Brazil is larger than the United States minus Alaska and has half of the population, with 130 million. It is heavily influenced by French and German culture, and has the largest Japanese population outside of Japan. According to Elenora Mendonca, Brazilian and South American women's marathon record holder (2:48:45), Brazilians are a very outdoor people because of the tropical weather, and take great pride in the way they look. Therefore physical activity is part of the national character.

However, because of the weather and geography, running is difficult in Brazil, and Elenora believes this is why there isn't a good tradition of Brazilian distance runners. Even track running, modeled on the European club system, is still only marginally developed. Elenora did graduate work in Boston, where she remains half the year to train and "to imitate and learn from the American system" for both her own running and race organizing in South America.

In 1978, after organizing a race in Brazil with 600 men and women, Elenora developed a road race calendar with events from 5 kilometers to the marathon, including special races for children. Women's running has grown tremendously since this time. In 1982, 5,330 ran an all-women's race in Brasília, and in 1983, 6,500 women ran a 10-kilometer in São Paulo, making it not only one of the largest women's road races in the world, but one of the largest for women or men. "Believe it or not," she says, "women are keeping up with men in the development of road running. The interest is there. Give women in Brazil the opportunity, and they will participate."

ENGLAND

While women's sports in the United States, specifically running, have been affected by a particular social movement, other countries have traditions in women's athletics which predate American influence by decades. England is a country with a good tradition of elite women distance runners, and although it does not yet compare with the United States as a movement for the masses, it is gaining ground.

According to Paula MacKenzie Newnham, a 24-year-old Commonwealth Games competitor for England in 1978 (2:02 for the half mile), women's running is part of the specialization in English society. "We do have a consistency for top runners not yet built in America; a woman has the same club and the same coach for years. English society is very specialized. You go to one type of school, take a specific type of exams, and are tracked for one type of profession. In England you're either a runner, a housewife, or a businesswoman, but certainly not all of them."

Mass sport is a separate division in this more specialized society. It is not done competitively, but rather socially, and is built around the English slogan "sport for all." Popular recreational women's sports include field hockey, netball, and badminton. It is with these activities that the masses engage in their sports tradition.

A basic difference exists between women's sports in England and America. Says Paula, "It is American feminism that encourages the average woman to think about herself and her fitness, and to feel she can do it all. There's a tremendous expectancy in the U.S.A.; a woman is supposed to be able to do everything. In England it is difficult to be serious about being fit without being a top athlete. The attitude is that sport should not infringe on other priorities."

Americans and the English differ in several other fundamental ways, one of the most important being the emphasis on the body. "There's a big preoccupation with weight in America we don't have in England." America stands alone in the degree of its fixation on thinness for women, the prime motivation for its exercise mania.

Yet more and more English women are taking to the roads. Priscilla

Welch is one of them. In 1980 at age 36 she ran her first marathon in 3:26. By 1983 she had become one of England's best, with 2:32:31. In its brief three-year history, the 1983 London Marathon drew 1,577 women, while several thousand competed in the four Avon races held the same year. These races, and distance running for the masses, which is being cultivated by such people as former English Olympian Brendan Foster, will help create a mass running movement for women if there is to be one. As in every country, however, there's a long way to go. "Top women runners like Joyce Smith and Wendy Sly are accepted for who they are," claims Paula, "but not a lot of women are emulating women athletes."

IRELAND

The day of the Evening Press/Brooks Women's Mini Marathon, with 8,000 entrants—the largest women's race in history—Irish journalist Con Houlighan wrote an article about the event, and his words about women in Ireland can be applied to women everywhere. "In this country and indeed in most countries—the women, whether ordinary or extraordinary, looked on athletics as a domain for the men . . . A generation ago you would meet the odd girl out running in the morning—or in the evening: most deemed them very odd . . . All, all is changed—an alarming beauty is born . . . They will go far beyond the merely physical—mass running will help to break the caste system that is one of the curses of Irish society. And it will help to bring down the wall between the sexes—in Ireland they have long been looked on as almost distinct species."*

ISRAEL

"When will the craziness pass?" jokingly ask friends of Zehava Shmueli, Israel's national record holder in the marathon. She was a 20-year-old mother of two when she started jogging for enjoyment. Seven years later, and despite being without competitive opportunities in her own country, Zehava has qualified to represent Israel in the 1984 Olympic Games marathon.

*"A Drift of Fine Women," *Irish Runner*, vol. 3, no. 5. pp. 10–18. August 1983.

She is one of the select women runners in countries throughout the world in which being a woman runner is nothing less than sheer struggle. "Women outside Israel admire me," says Zehava, a woman whose talent has been tested only in a handful of marathons to which she has been invited or sent by her sports federation, "but in Israel they ask, 'How can a mother of two have a sports career?'" One of only two serious women marathoners in her country—the other being her sister Mazal, a 2:55 marathoner—Zehava came in eighth in the 1982 Boston Marathon—her 2:44 a personal best by six minutes, which she improved to 2:40 in her next try in the 1983 London Marathon.

Life was relatively quiet on the collective farm, called a *Moshav*, where Zehava Shalom was raised as one of five children. Like most women in her Sephardic culture and many others in her country, she finished high school and was married early, at age 18, thereby becoming exempt from mandatory military service.

She was an average Israeli housewife until she discovered running, in which she remembers excelling even in childhood. Although she ran alone and with no social or personal support, she says she was motivated by "my enjoyment as well as quick results." But in a country in which inflation was 191 percent in 1983, the highest in the world, and where war and volatile political and social issues constantly undermine stability, getting anywhere in sports has not been easy for Zehava. "We are much more directly affected by everything that happens in Israel than people are in other countries. Every top athlete—whether a student, soldier, or part of a married couple—has difficulties, both social and financial."

Her husband used to feel her running was physically dangerous, but now she says he supports her, accompanying her on long runs on a bicycle with water and encouragement. But she's still alone at the top. Zehava's situation would surely be helped, and in turn so would that of Israeli women, if others took up the sport. Says Zehava, however, "Although there's a little interest among women running for fun and fitness, there is none for competition. It's going to take a lot of brainwashing to get any number of women in races in Israel."

Meanwhile, living in suburban Tel Aviv, she must juggle the care of her sons and her family finances in a country whose economy changes almost daily. While sports such as soccer and tennis are given unlimited support, Zehava receives only a token $50 a month for her position on the national Olympic team. "Fifty dollars," she says sarcastically, "really, I ask you. . . ."

JAPAN

It would seem hard to imagine women runners in a country with the strictest separation between male and female roles. Japan is associated with its tradition of quiet and docile women. Yet Japanese women athletes are notoriously tough (like the Olympic champion volleyball team) and the number of women participating in Japanese road races has often been unparalleled. The famous Eikeden Relay, for example, which took place on March 6, 1983, drew 1,255 women. Other women's events, from 5 kilometers to the marathon, commonly attract from 500 to 800 women.

Akemi Masuda sets the pace of Japanese women's running, literally and figuratively. At 19 years old, this national marathon champion is also the world junior record holder, with her 2:30:20 clocking in the Nike-OTC Marathon in Oregon in September, 1983, which was broadcast on Japanese television. Racing side by side with Western men was understandably a culture shock, expecially for such a small woman—so young and so far from home. Yet tiny Masuda (4 feet 10 inches, 80 pounds) is as tough as nails. Japan's top male runners testify that she can hold her own running even with them.

Men and women never race together in Japan's major events. Popular Japanese ladies' marathons like the Tokyo Ladies Marathon and the Osaka Ladies Marathon are broadcast on television to the entire nation. Ironically, these races are major Japanese spectator sporting events, so for a day the women own the roads and the attention of all Japan, illustrating the absurdity of the tradition which requires them to remain subservient and unseen.

Masuda, who has as much as two decades of development ahead of her and the possibility of four Olympic Games, lives the seemingly incongruous life of both an elite runner and a Japanese woman. Her training consists of an astronomical 150 miles per week, a work load that would be envied even among the world's top male runners, which is combined with stretching, exercises, and the acupuncturist pins for healing or injury prevention that are painfully inserted into her able muscles.

Yet she shifts gears in social situations. Like all Japanese women, she speaks only when addressed or to frequently apologize or express continual thanks for seemingly nothing. As a runner she is number one, but because of Japanese custom, in social situations she is relegated to last as she is a woman and often the youngest in a gathering.

Yet Masuda is still an exception. Most Japanese women her age have their minds on marriage instead of mileage, or a rare few contemplate the extremely difficult college entrance exams. Racing among married women or single women of marriageable age is seldom seen in Japan. Only one female runner of note is married (a hurdler). Two older single women excel in track events, one of whom is a very rare exception at 31 years old.

If these talented Japanese woman runners are given as much respect for their achievements as they in turn are required to show in their society, a running boom may yet arrive.

NEW ZEALAND AND AUSTRALIA

Gabriella van der Fluit is one of the millions of New Zealanders who was raised with a love of sport, particularly distance running, and she has kept up her training during her travels around the world.

After running through the streets of such major cities as Paris, Brussels, Amsterdam, and New York, she claims nothing compares to the freedom of running in New Zealand. "In Australia and the United States, there's always the hooting, the comments, or being pinched on the behind. I remember being frightened by it at first. This has never happened to me in New Zealand."

Gabriella postulates that the popularity of distance running in New Zealand is connected to the history of that pioneer land, settled by mostly Scottish, English, and Irish emigrants who came on their own accord and worked their own plot of land. "They were happy with enough," she says. "Individual achievement was important, and they had a love of doing physical things with their own power and strength."

Yet despite this attitude, top New Zealand runner Anne Audain complains that the elite women have traditionally lacked the opportunities the men had to travel outside the country to compete. She claims that this lack of competition held her back, and that she would have fared better had she been an American or European athlete. Says Anne, "It's a very male-oriented society, and although the women are now enjoying the most success, the opportunities still aren't there for them." But on one point perhaps no New Zealander would argue. "I do think the one thing the system does is make you very tough. You either make it or you don't. There's no in-between."

The way women are viewed in certain situations is significant as a cultural comparison, claims Gabriella. "In New Zealand there are no cheer girls like in American football. Female sexuality is not a side show at a game or a rugby match. In America everyone waits for the girls to come out shaking their behinds." Finally, she says, "In New Zealand a female athlete is admired for what she can do as an athlete rather than as a woman."

The situation in Australia is baffling. The Aussies boast a tradition of many of the greatest male distance runners in history, such as Herb Elliot, Ron Clarke, Derek Clayton, and Rob de Castella—presently the best marathoner in the world. Yet the Australian women's national record was only 2:37:12 until December, 1983, when Australian Lisa Martin, a resident of Oregon, set a new record of 2:32:22. Especially considering the quality of Australia's male runners, these times compare poorly with 2:22:43 for the United States; 2:25:29 for New Zealand and Norway, and sub-2:30 times for England, Ireland, Canada, and Germany. Women's participation in Australian races is also far below that of many other countries.

Gabriella is proud of the many women distance runners in New Zealand, but when asked about notable women runners in Australia, where she once lived, she says with a laugh, "The only Australian woman of note who comes to mind is Olivia Newton-John." Seeing the need for a running movement in Australia, she plans to move there soon in hopes of organizing road races, a skill she has been learning in the United States.

Part II
A Runner's Body:
What Women Want to Know

There is probably somebody born every minute who has all the machinery
to be a great athlete in one form or another.

Dr. David L. Costill, exercise physiologist,
The Runner, *September 1983*

"K NOW THYSELF," said Socrates, and nothing could be truer for what women runners want in regard to their bodies. And there is no knowledge more desired, or more essential, than understanding how we physically perform and respond to our sport, and how running in turn affects our bodies.

Of the many areas of medical, physiological, and psychological interest to women, this chapter deals with those which are of special importance to women runners, and about which they express the greatest interest. In the L'eggs Mini Marathon survey, medical aspects were ranked as almost two times more important than other major topics on women's running.

The purpose of this chapter is not scientific analysis, but to familiarize women with recent discoveries about those sometimes mysterious, and always controversial, aspects of their athletic biology.

In response to the growth of women's sports, the field of sports gynecology was created to accommodate many of the woman athlete's special needs and problems. However, since this field is so new, so is research in this area. A review of the articles on the subject of medical aspects of women's running reveals mainly what is *not* known about the hows and whys of certain physical responses to strenuous training. For every statement of fact on the subject, there seems to be a contradiction, and for every supposition, another question. It is hoped that much of the present research being conducted in these controversial areas will provide new answers. And current research includes not only physical effects on women runners, but infertility in male runners, which is also being tested.

One thing we can be sure of is that the myths of women needing to avoid exercise are just that—myths. Women need not shun exercise during any phase of the menstrual cycle, or even pregnancy. And pound for pound, muscle for muscle, women are every bit as able as men to withstand the most strenuous training.

A 1980 opinion of the American College of Sports Medicine states: "Females should not be denied the opportunity to compete in long-distance running. There exists no conclusive scientific or medical evidence that long-distance running is contraindicated for the healthy, trained female athlete. The American College of Sports Medicine recommends that females be allowed to compete at the national and international level in the same distances in which their male counterparts compete."

11

Menstruation

THE MENSTRUAL CYCLE influences almost every part of the body, including the psyche, skin, thermoregulatory system, and gastrointestinal tract. It stands to reason, therefore, that we wonder how menstruation affects athletic participation, and vice versa. Both positive and negative results on athletic performance have been attributed to menstruation, but a number of studies show there is no definite effect on performance, which varies with the individual. Some women claim it is detrimental to performance, while others find it has little effect. It is well publicized that women have won Olympic gold medals at all phases of the menstrual cycle.

In fact, many women report an improvement of menstrual function with exercise. In many cases, exercise regulates the cycle and alleviates menstrual cramps. It is speculated that this could be the result of improved blood circulation in the uterus, distraction from the discomfort, or the result of a higher pain threshold a woman may have developed through exercise. The exercise may also be releasing endorphins—natural painkillers, which alleviate menstrual discomfort.

MENSTRUAL IRREGULARITY

One of the topics of greatest current interest is the incidence of menstrual irregularity in women runners. Before we consider menstrual changes which can occur in active women, several brief definitions are instructive.

Normal Menstruation occurs every 25 to 32 days. A cycle that occurs every 20 to 60 days need not be evaluated by a doctor unless a woman wishes to become pregnant.

Oligomenorrhea refers to a continuation of menstruation, but at intervals greater than 35 days. *Amenorrhea* means a woman has fewer than three periods a year.

Although this subject is the focus of much attention, it is estimated that fewer than 20 percent of the approximately 22 million exercising women in the United States will have menstrual dysfunction. It should be emphasized that experts all agree there is no reason for a woman to refrain from participation in any athletic activity due to any of these menstrual conditions, and there is no concrete evidence to show that a missed or absent cycle in a runner is dangerous, or that the condition is usually more than temporary.

According to the American College of Sports Medicine, approximately one-third of competitive women long-distance runners between the ages of 12 and 45 experience menstrual dysfunction (amenorrhea or oligomennorrhea) for at least brief intervals. But other estimates range anywhere from 0 percent to 50 percent of athletic women experiencing dysfunction. There are several widely believed theories as to why it occurs, but in a review of over twenty-five articles on the subject, most conclusions were based on single, limited studies, and many of the studies contradicted each other. The most commonly cited causes attributed to dysfunction are weight loss, low body fat, and stress. Other contributing factors predisposing female athletes to amenorrhea are prior menstrual dysfunction, delayed menarche (onset of menstruation), and emotional stress.

Some studies linked amenorrhea to certain specific age groups, and the condition does appear to occur more often among younger women. One study found that menstrual dysfunction occurred in women ages 24.3 plus or minus 1.3 years, while regular menstrual cycles were found in women 31.4 plus or minus 1.3 years.* The study also claimed that younger runners were more prone to develop the condition directly as a result of running. However, Susan Cushman of the Melpomene Institute, which studies women athletes, believes that the stress incurred by college-age women runners due to a new routine and added pressure is responsible for their 25 to 50 percent rate of amenorrhea. In her study of 400 women in the Boston Marathon and Bonne Belle 10-kilometer race, only 3.4 percent had the condition.

Prior pregnancy seems to aid in preventing menstrual dysfunction,

---

* Baker, Elizabeth R., M.D., "Menstrual Dysfunction and Hormonal Status in Athletic Women: A Review," *Fertility & Sterility*, vol. 36, no. 6, pp. 691–95.

according to several experts. Another study claimed that the longer or faster a woman ran, the greater the likelihood of dysfunction. Another said that 40 percent of women who run 80-plus miles a week become amenorrheic, and that the amenorrehic women are faster runners than those menstruating regularly. Because these findings are based on single studies, undoubtedly no authority would be willing to draw conclusions from them, and most would probably refute their validity as generalities.

Despite evidence that links body fat, weight loss, and training to menstrual dysfunction, the presence of many other factors complicates proving this correlation. For example, menstrual dysfunction was found in women cadets in their first year at West Point, which was caused by a combination of physical and emotional stress. Emotional stress can result in a delay of the onset of menstrual problems six to twelve months following the incidence of stress, making evaluation of the cause of dysfunction even more complicated. Flight attendants have been found to experience menstrual dysfunction from intercontinental trips, and it is claimed that obesity can also depress menstruation.

Although some believe that amenorrhea is prevalent in women who run hard and are thin as a result, some studies claim that weight, body fat, and weekly mileage are just a part of the story. It is difficult to assign a general cause to the condition, one study claimed, because every woman is different. This study found that less than one-fourth of the women athletes tested had both low weight and high mileage.* Based on these and other contrary findings, the authors recommend that physicians seek explanations other than running when evaluating menstrual dysfunction. The study emphasizes that in fact female athletes respond favorably to the demands of endurance exercise.

In most cases, menstruation returns with a decrease in training or a decrease in the intensity of training. Whereas body fat levels of 22 to 29 percent are normal for sedentary women, runners are far below these percentages. Some experts say it is necessary to return to 22 percent or higher to reinitiate menstruation, but Dr. Mona Shangold says that this number is being challenged. Many women with low body fat continue to have periods, and many fat women don't have periods, she points out. Dr. Shangold, an acknowledged expert on the subject of women runners, is assistant professor of obstetrics and gynecology at Georgetown University School of Medicine, and coauthor of the forthcoming *The Complete Sportsmedicine Book for Women.*

It has been pointed out that reproductive function ceases in mammals

---

*Mahle Lutter, Judy, M.A., and Susan Cushman. "Menstrual Patterns in Female Runners," *The Physician and Sports Medicine*, vol. 10, no. 9, pp. 60–72, September 1982.

when environmental circumstances are unfavorable. This is the case in certain animal species, and in humans during times of famine. Therefore, the cessation of menstruation may be a natural reaction against a condition for which the athlete's body is temporarily unsuited.

Although there is no proof that athletic amenorrhea is harmful, gynecologists recommend an examination to assure that the condition is not caused by a more serious dysfunction. Dr. Shangold recommends that if amenorrhea is present for one year or more, an estrogen-progesterone regimen should be undergone to prevent vascular problems, osteoporosis (bone loss), and stress fractures, and to protect the lining of the uterus and the function of the ovaries—all affected by the absence or inadequate balance of female hormones.

Women should be aware that the absence of menstruation does not mean they are protected from pregnancy. Some amenorrheic women runners, believing the condition a natural form of birth control, have been surprised to find themselves pregnant.

Dr. Shangold reports that many women runners don't seek the counsel of a doctor regarding amenorrhea because they claim they are just as happy not to menstruate. "I don't believe that," she says. "I don't think they're being honest with themselves. Menstruation is intertwined with femininity. A regular cycle is a sign that the body is working normally and athletes, of all people, are more attuned to the body." She points out that there is a difference between the convenience of not bleeding for competition and not menstruating at all. In addition, Shangold stresses the importance of an examination because she believes that amenorrhea is connected to bone problems such as stress fractures.

However, testimony of a number of amenorrheic runners reveals that at least psychologically they feel no need to experience their period. Dr. Joan Ullyot, physician, runner, and writer, gives them even more reason to feel at ease with the absence of their periods. "My advice to runners with amenorrhea is, don't worry about it," she writes. "Don't be frightened into thinking that a woman has to bleed monthly to be healthy. Since amenorrhea is so common in fit, healthy young runners, whereas clockwork-like menstrual cycles are more frequent in the sedentary, plump population, I have developed what I call my 'anthropological theory of the origin of monthly cycles.'"

Ullyot theorizes that anthropologically speaking, monthly periods are a phenomenon of a society with reduced activity, a physiological aberration, and the result of life in an inactive society in which sedentary women have higher percentages of body fat. She points out that in countries such as India, where the population is leaner, menstruation begins at age 15 or

16, versus age 11 in the United States. She suggests that if a woman wants to get pregnant, she should first try cutting out birth control for up to a year, then cutting stress and gaining some body fat, and only if these measures fail, going to a gynecologist.

Top runner Kiki Sweigart (a 2:36 marathoner) is one of those who is satisfied to leave her condition as it is. Amenorrheic for the past eight years, she stopped having her period in college, even before she took up running. She claims she genuinely does not long to menstruate just for the sake of having a regular cycle. She did once try to stabilize her hormones, but the physical discomfort of the unexpected period it induced caused her to stop. She says that although the doctor believed it was harmful for her to be without her period, she argued that it wasn't proven and she didn't want to play with her body. Other amenorrheic women runners have adamantly said they would not have their periods induced.

MENSTRUAL DISCOMFORT

Menstrual cramps are caused by substances in the body called prostaglandins, chemicals that make the muscle of the uterus contract, resulting in discomfort. Aspirin will help alleviate the pain, but if it is severe enough to cause disruption of a woman's routine, prescription drugs which inhibit prostaglandins are available. Nutritionist Randi Aaron suggests as an alternative to drugs that various amounts of vitamin B6, calcium, and magnesium may lessen symptoms. Running or exercise need not be avoided, and often helps relieve the cramps.

Premenstrual Syndrome (PMS) occurs before the beginning of menstruation, and can take the form of anxiety, depression, swelling (fluid retention), increased appetite, acne, and a craving for sweets. It is caused by hormonal fluctuations, and although the cause of PMS is the same for athletes and nonathletes, some women runners may notice a heavy feeling in their legs when they run. A survey revealed that 50 to 75 percent of athletic women experience PMS symptoms, although exercise may lessen them. Moderate mood changes are normal with PMS, but extreme mood swings may be helped by consulting a gynecologist. Some suggest that a careful diet, avoiding excess salt and sugar (especially during PMS), may lessen some of its symptoms.

12

Pregnancy

RUNNING AND PREGNANCY is a subject about which there are many unknowns, and much controversy. What is certain, however, is the tremendous interest this new topic has generated, resulting in scores of inquiries of the medical profession. One recently published study begins by reminding us, "Twenty years ago the exercise prescription for a pregnant woman was safe and easy: walk or work in the garden." Today, like all women's sports issues, it is much more complicated.

Experts agree that it is unreasonable to expect the active woman to completely give up her lifestyle during pregnancy. But running during pregnancy, an activity whose physical and psychological consequences have raised emotional debate, requires caution and special consideration.

It has long been believed that being fit has its advantages for childbearing. In ancient Sparta, women participated in athletics, as it was said this better prepared them for motherhood. According to Plato, only strong and physically fit women could give birth to healthy and robust children. In the U.S.S.R., scientific investigations show that long-term training has eased childbirth.

However, an active woman may understandably feel caught between her athletic life and her desire to have a safe pregnancy. She wants to know if she can continue to run, how much or how hard, and for how long. According to medical experts, with caution and conservative pace and mileage, a fit woman can continue her running during pregnancy. The shaking and bouncing, which are obvious concerns, pose no risk, as the baby is well protected inside the mother during all phases of pregnancy.

Evidence shows that exercising may be good for the mother. Some fit women are better able to tolerate the strenuous work load of labor and delivery than unfit women. One study revealed that compared to nonexercising women, a majority of those who continued exercise throughout pregnancy had a decrease in the incidence of toxemia, the rate of cesarean section, and a diminished duration for the second stage of labor.

Some of the common reasons cited in a *Physician and Sports Medicine* article for exercising during pregnancy are "1. to control weight gain, 2. to decrease backache, 3. to decrease "postpartum belly," 4. to decrease varicose veins, 5. to decrease constipation, 6. to increase energy to enjoy daily life, 7. to sleep better at night, 8. to decrease daily tension, 9. to improve appearance, especially posture, 10. to be better able to cope with the physical stress of pregnancy."

Exercise may be good for the mother, but little is known about its effects on the fetus. In order to determine what they might be, one must consider the normal physiological changes which occur during pregnancy: increased heart rate and blood volume, joint laxity (softening), and decreased respiratory reserve. These changes affect a woman's ability to exercise, and the fetus as well. Yet by allowing for them, and with a doctor's supervision, a woman can run through pregnancy safely. Although the results have not yet been analyzed, in a study of 1,500 pregnant women, 100 of whom were runners, it is the opinion of the researcher that no deleterious effects occur in offspring of runners versus nonrunners.

Certain guidelines should be followed for the woman who plans to continue running during pregnancy. It is the expressed opinion of the American College of Obstetrics and Gynecology that any exercise recommendation during pregnancy should be based on an individual woman's medical and exercise history, and any complications encountered in the pregnancy. A woman should consult her gynecologist about running while pregnant, and continuation of the activity should be based on a problem-free pregnancy.

Women are urged to get in shape before becoming pregnant. They can usually continue activity on a regular basis during the first and second trimesters, but during the third trimester there is a gradual decrease in physical efficiency. Running or exercising in the final stages is up to the individual, but it is likely a time to do only light exercise.

California chiropractor Dr. Leroy Perry, Jr., supports running through the early stages of pregnancy, but believes that running during the third trimester causes too much bouncing and, together with the added weight, disrupts the body's biomechanics. Perry, who did half his internship in obstetrics and delivered his own four children at home, suggests running in a swimming pool in the later stages of pregnancy, which decreases spinal stress and gravity compression on the spine. He reports his wife ran in a pool until the day before the birth of her fourth child. All exercise, he emphasizes, should be done with the obstetrician's approval.

Until more research is done on the subject, strenuous running during pregnancy should be avoided, and all exercise should be approached with caution. According to an article in *The Physician and Sports Medicine*, serious training, including competition, can be resumed five to six weeks post-partum.

Some trained women might continue to run while not knowing they are in the early stages of pregnancy. As there is a concern over oxygen and blood deprivation to the fetus, and the possibility that an increase in body temperature may potentially cause birth defects, one doctor recommends planning pregnancy if possible and reducing activity during the first six to eight weeks.

Dr. Shangold suggests checking for overheating of the body during pregnancy by taking the body temperature after running. If it is above 101 degrees Fahrenheit, steps should be taken to keep cooler by running with lighter clothing and during a cooler time of day, drinking more water, or slowing the pace.

Some researchers have pointed out that pregnancy is part of an entire female biological cycle that proves women have a great capacity for adaptation, such as that needed for heavy athletic training. Women's Olympic track coach Brooks Johnson believes, "Because women are constitutionally suited to go through childbirth, they are superior in many respects. They have a higher pain threshold and undergo stress better than men."

Kathy Horton, a 2:48 marathoner, was 35 years old when she had her first child, who came into the world having logged 40 to 50 miles of running a week during her mother's pregnancy. While Kathy was up and walking around a day after the birth, she noticed the doctors couldn't even rouse most of the younger women out of bed.

Running while pregnant didn't feel greatly different, according to Kathy. "I felt as if the baby were a part of me—like an arm or a leg." Like other women who have comfortably and successfully run while pregnant, her most emphatic advice is to listen to the body as a guideline.

This is also the advice of Sue Crowe, who has run through two pregnancies, during which her 70-mile-per-week running was modified to 3 to 5 miles a day. If she didn't feel good, she didn't run, or she interspersed walking with running.

Neither woman is willing to say whether her relatively easy delivery had anything to do with running, but both claim they felt better psychologically—"just to get out and do something," as Sue puts it. Running suited these women, but some women report running while pregnant just didn't feel right, and so they took up other methods of exercise.

Several interesting and unexpected things happened to both these women as a result of running while pregnant. Mainly because she was amenorrheic, Sue did not realize she was pregnant with her first child for six months, and continued to run, and race, 60 to 70 miles a week. Although it sounds quite strenuous, Sue felt almost nothing. "I don't think it harmed me because I don't overpush myself when I don't feel right," she says. She felt only slightly tired, and gained a small amount of weight during this time, which she attributed to a change of location and diet. Is it possible to run through six months of pregnancy and not realize it? The answer is yes, according to Dr. Shangold, who has seen it happen before. "It depends on where your mind is," she says. "If you're looking to get pregnant, you'll notice; if not, you may ignore the symptoms."

If Kathy Horton had any problems running while pregnant, they weren't physical, but social. "The worst part about it was the negative comments from complete strangers. They horrified me with questions like, 'Aren't you afraid your baby will be born retarded?' I just told them I was running with the approval of my doctor," says Kathy.

People seemed especially upset when they saw her running through a 4-mile race at a 7:30-per-mile pace. But Kathy points out that for someone like herself who is trained to run at a sub-6-minute pace, a 7:30 mile is as harmless as a 10-minute mile for someone else.

On the other hand, some runners expected too much of her, or misunderstood her motivation to run while pregnant. "Are you going to run the marathon?" they asked her, and to Kathy's shock, they often expressed the belief that she was running to prevent weight gain. So upset was she by the impression that she was trying to keep her weight down that she ate extra helpings, even when she wasn't particularly hungry.

Both women's examples illustrate a need for understanding of the subject by all concerned—the pregnant runner herself, her running peers, and sedentary society. But the most important education is that of the pregnant woman herself. She must be careful not to "train through" pregnancy. Says Dr. David Leaf, who has studied pregnant women runners, "Having a baby is a significant life event. Listen to your body. Go your own pace."

Another issue of pregnancy is the conflict a woman athlete experiences over becoming pregnant in the first place—changing her lifestyle, and significantly, her self-image. Sports psychology specialist Linda Lewis Griffith finds that women athletes often experience conflicts over childbirth because becoming heavy disturbs their body image. How to deal with pregnancy psychologically may become an important issue as women athletes are actively competing at later ages, and often indefinitely.

"There's still one more thing I should do, want to do," says top runner Kiki Sweigart. The one thing for 32-year-old Kiki is having a baby, but is it "should" or "want"? "A little of both," she admits. The "want" is that she does love children—she's been a teacher for eleven years—and the "should" is that she feels she owes it to her husband, Ray, to have their own baby, rather than adopt as she might have wished. "He's not pressuring me, but I know someday he wants his own family. He's been very supportive of what I want to do." This much is true: no husband is better at supporting his wife's running than Ray Sweigart, Kiki's husband of nine years.

But in principle Kiki would rather adopt because she says, "Being pregnant doesn't give me any thrill. You hear, 'It's an experience you have to go through.' Well, why?" Is getting heavy for the ultra-thin and muscular Kiki what disturbs her about being pregnant? "I suppose it's in the back of my mind. It's a mental process that fights getting fat. I'll always think about getting fat; it's part of my system.

"I'm not happy getting that way, but when I want a baby, I'm willing to accept it. And I've always felt I'll know deep down inside when I want one." Kiki rightly points out that even women who don't run have to adjust to becoming fat during pregnancy.

Even for such a physical person as Kiki, the physical aspects of giving birth hold no interest. Childbirth is innate, but running challenges her. "Having a baby is a physical ability you're born with. The physicalness of running is something you work hard for, something you put your mind to." There's still some running she's got to do before she thinks about getting pregnant. "When I feel I've run the best I can run, then I'll be ready." But every woman who identifies with her wonders if that day of readiness will ever arrive.

Kiki must consider the physical as well as psychological problems of pregnancy. Although she is amenorrheic, she feels she would be faced with the difficulty of getting pregnant even without running. Her sister, thin and amenorrheic, had difficulty, and she didn't run a step. "If I have to take drugs to try and get pregnant, and feel miserable in the process, I won't do it. If I can't have a baby the way God intended it, it won't be done."

13

Birth Control

OBVIOUSLY, an active woman will be more affected, and therefore more concerned, by the birth control she uses. However, the two contraceptive methods with the highest rate of effectiveness and the easiest to use, the birth control pill and the IUD, are also the object of the most complaints and criticism for their side effects by both sedentary and active women.

In several studies of women runners, the pill and the IUD were the least used contraceptive methods. Side effects suffered by 40 percent of all pill-taking women are probably a good reason why. Included among these disadvantages are weight gain, fatigue, depression, and vitamin deficiencies—all particularly troublesome to women runners. In fact, the pill affects virtually every organ system in the body.

Dr. Mona Shangold's survey of women in the 1979 New York City Marathon revealed that the largest percentage of marathoners (37 percent) used the diaphragm. Only 6 percent took the pill, and 16 percent used the IUD. Sterilization, or no method at all, made up the additional percentages. She feels, however, that the risks and side effects are fewer in the newer low-dose birth control pills.

A recent study at the University of Illinois found that of 70 women runners, only 13 percent used the pill, as opposed to 44 percent for the diaphragm. The common complaint among runners that the pill makes them feel slow and sluggish may now be substantiated. Findings from a small-scale study show that the pill can cause "considerable" reduction in maximum oxygen uptake (VO_2 max) in athletes. A drop in VO_2 max of 18 to 19 percent occurred in pill-taking runners, while a group not on the pill experienced no change. Six weeks after the women went off the pill, their VO$_2$ max returned to normal. There are indications, however, that after twelve months on the pill, the body begins to acclimatize. But that's "rather a long time to wait," concludes the researcher.

The IUD has caused problems for women runners, especially because of heavy bleeding. There is also a risk of infection from the device, which if contracted can cause permanent damage to the reproductive organs. Therefore, Dr. Shangold does not recommend an IUD for childless women who may want to have children in the future.

Some women object to the intrusion of any method that remains inside the body. For those women, a possible alternative is the use of a condom, or for a statistical efficiency rate as high as the other methods, a condom and contraceptive foam used together.

14

Breasts

RUNNING has little direct effect on the breasts. In fact, in an informal poll of 27 marathoners, chafing was the only breast injury reported. Breast size is based on heredity and body fat, and since breasts are composed mostly of fat, one result of running may be a decrease in breast size which occurs with general weight loss, particularly of body fat. Breast size has no medical or physical implication, only a psychological one, and a significant factor is that running favors a smaller-breasted woman.

Running, even without a bra, will not necessarily cause breasts to sag, although running braless may be uncomfortable. Yet there is no evidence that running braless is harmful, and some smaller-breasted women prefer to run without one. If nipple irritation occurs, however, Vaseline or Band-Aids can help.

Bras should be supportive, and some women prefer a specially designed running or sports bra. A bra should be comfortable, but not so tight that it interferes with breathing. If the bra causes chafing, try Vaseline as a preventive measure. (See "Running Gear" for details on bras.)

According to Dr. Leroy Perry, who treats both Olympic-caliber and weekend athletes, the way a woman carries her arms often affects her posture, and therefore her biomechanics while running.

Some women carry their arms improperly while running. Because improper arm swing can result from poor biomechanics, and can in turn injure the breasts by inadvertently hitting them, Perry urges awareness of proper arm swing: a back-and-forth pendulum motion as opposed to a rotary movement in which the arms swing around the body.

While smaller-breasted women can choose not to wear a bra, Perry believes it is mechanically inefficient for any woman of significant breast size to run braless. Having designed various bras for Olympic and professional athletes, he recommends a style that flattens the breasts against the rib cage.

15

Bone Disorders

ONE OF THE MOST recent areas of inquiry deals with the speculation that amenorrheic women may be suffering from osteoporosis (bone loss) and therefore are more prone to stress fractures. According to Dr. Christopher Cann of the University of California, San Francisco, one of the causes of osteoporosis is the low amount of estrogen present in the bodies of amenorrheic women. In a test of these women, he found less bone mass than he considered normal. Although studies have shown that exercise increases bone density, its loss in amenorrheic women may override any of these exercise gains. In addition to calcium and vitamin D, Dr. Cann has prescribed small doses of estrogen to some of the women in his study, although he cautions against its long-term use in young women.

For bone maintenance, it is important for women to have adequate calcium in the diet, which can be obtained from milk products. The recommended dose of calcium for menstruating women is 1,000 milligrams a day, and 1,500 milligrams for menopausal women. Yet on any given day, half the women in the United States over 15 are consuming no more than three-fourths the Recommended Daily Allowance for calcium, and after age 35, 75 percent of the women are below the minimum requirement of 800 milligrams.

Other experts, however, attribute bone problems to different causes. One is the sudden change in women from nonathletic to athletic lifestyles. Cardiovascular fitness is achieved relatively quickly, but muscles, and especially bones, take a longer amount of time to adapt to increased exercise.

Tibial stress reaction or actual stress fractures appear to be more common in women. In a West Point survey, 10 percent of the women cadets developed stress fractures after beginning a running program. According to noted sports medicine specialist Dr. Dorothy Harris, osteoporosis occurs for reasons of socialization. If girls are encouraged to participate earlier and more often in vigorous exercise, she says, they will develop stronger and denser bones. The conclusion of some experts is that a gradual increase in athletic activity for women will result in no more stress fractures than a male would incur.

While Dr. Shangold and other experts believe there is a correlation between ammenorrhea and bone problems, Judy Mahle Lutter, president of the Melpomene Institute, believes bone loss in amenorrheic athletes is a long way from being proved. The women in Dr. Cann's study, several top Stanford University runners among them, expressed a wait-and-see attitude about the findings on bone loss, its possible cause by amenorrhea, and treatment for the condition.

16

What Other Specialists Have to Say

A PHYSICAL THERAPIST

"I never used to need to tell a woman runner to take time off from training; now I do." These are the words of New York physical therapist Peter Marshall, a favorite among both runners and dancers. Now that "women runners are every bit as serious as men," in his words, they must deal with an extensive range of athletic injuries.

According to Marshall, because most women lack background knowledge in muscle strengthening, they tend to have problems in handling running mileage. "Many women have very weak quadricep muscles—they're surprised when I tell them just how weak," says Marshall. He stresses that no matter what level of runner, these weak muscles can cause problems, and urges women to do exercises for the quadriceps (front thigh muscles), which are not strengthened by running itself. He also suggests that the relative newness of women participating in the sport may be a contributing factor to what he finds is another common cause of injury—women increasing their mileage too soon.

Ready or not, here's what Peter Marshall hears all the time: women are afraid to do the exercises for their leg muscles because they worry about getting big thighs. He stresses how unfortunate this reluctance is, because the exercises give tightness, not bulk, and they are extremely important, especially among previously sedentary women who don't have the muscle strength to handle the mileage—no matter how little or how much they run.

On the plus side, women do have better flexibility than men, according to Marshall, with a higher percentage of elastic fibrous tissue and fibers in ligaments. Because women have more distensible (capable of being stretched) soft tissue, Marshall gets quicker results in programs he uses to make women more flexible by stretching, and they also respond more quickly to massage done to remove scar tissue.

With a combination of this flexibility and strengthening exercises, a woman runner can balance her athletic program and remain injury-free. Marshall's other reminder for injury prevention, especially for city runners, is to be aware of the shock-absorbent properties of shoes. "There's a big difference between running on concrete and asphalt or any other surface," he says. "Concrete is the worst."

Since Marshall sees so many athletes, and his job is to analyze their complete physical profile, how does he assess the body type of an elite woman runner? "Top runners are all cut out of the same mold—skinny, flat-chested, narrow-hipped, with good muscle definition." How do they get that way? "That's an unknown, but it's probably a combination of what they do, and what they're born with."

A CHIROPRACTOR

Dr. Leroy Perry, Jr., has treated athletes from 34 countries, and his patients have included such women runners as Mary Decker and Evelyn Ashford. Perry, who has been on hand at the Olympics and the World Championships, treats all levels of athletes and sedentary citizens alike.

His philosophy is based on kinetic therapy—muscle education therapy through motion, as well as an understanding of biomechanics. His aim is to aid athletes in developing proper posture through exercise—the key to successful and injury-free running. According to Perry, the greatest problem for women runners, as well as men, is simple bad posture.

Perry points out several areas of particular concern to women. One is the issue of proper upper body carriage and breast protection (discussed in Chapter 14). Another is the frequently referred to syndrome of wide hips, which has been said to predispose a woman runner to injury. According to Perry, wide hips as the cause of injury are not a genetic problem, but a result of weak abdominal and inner thigh muscles.

"This syndrome is not just exclusive to women, but for example includes overweight men, the types with beer bellies. It's just noticed on women because they're looked at more." Perry claims "postnatal spread" (the wide hips which remain after giving birth) is caused by not doing the proper exercises after childbirth to get the hips back where they belong.

He has developed what he calls "decompression exercises" specifically for this problem. And with good biomechanics, he claims, there's no reason a woman athlete will have a much wider pelvis than a male, if she uses her body properly. A look at most elite men and women athletes does in fact reveal they are both equally narrow-hipped.

Another problem area for both men and women is bad backs. "Eighty percent of those people with bad backs have the problem because their abdominals are weak and their backs are too strong. Strengthening the inner thighs and the abdomen takes pressure off the spine, and helps prevent injury."

Perry's approach to injury prevention and successful running is total body efficiency. "Good biomechanics means learning to use the back as well as the front of the body, and the inside as well as the outside." For more information on Dr. Perry's exercises and treatment techniques, see the Resource List.

A NUTRITIONIST

It wasn't very long ago that not many people thought much about what they ate—until the health-conscious sixties and the advent of the fitness movement, and until athletes and exercisers realized that what they eat has a direct effect on performance, as well as general health and well-being.

What to eat before a run or a race is critical. Many beginning runners think that food before a run will give them needed fuel, but quite the opposite is the case. Food is not only unnecessary before a run, but usually detrimental. One of the causes of cramps while running is eating too close to the time of activity. The general rule is to eat at least three hours before a run, and to keep in mind that protein and large meals take longer to digest. It is usually not a good idea to eat anything at all before a race. In prerace meals, roughage (e.g., fruits, vegetables, whole grain bread), spicy foods, and anything to which one is unaccustomed should be avoided. Many runners feel ready to go with just a cup of coffee, and some evidence shows the caffeine actually aids performance in certain cases. The benefits of carbohydrates or carbohydrate loading are realized only in runs or races of over two hours.

In her treatment of runners and swimmers, nutritionist and runner Randi Aaron has discovered certain patterns and common problems which she classifies into various types. If you fit any of the following categories, you should be aware that an active woman's nutritional needs are different from her sedentary counterpart's, and that your diet requires special care and consideration. These are the types of women Aaron counsels:

1. A woman who eats enough calories, but not the right kind. This is a woman who will eat things like frozen yogurt or ice cream, and forfeit the good foods.
2. A woman for whom weight loss is the goal, at the expense of everything. This is a malnourished woman who often walks a fine line between a high degree of training and anorexia.
3. A woman who has the knowledge, but doesn't take action. This woman is too lazy to make sure she eats a good diet.
4. A woman who doesn't know what diet is right. She is confused by the tremendous amount of information on food and diets.

Poor diet results in some common deficiencies for the woman athlete, and by the use of a computer, Randi Aaron can efficiently detect what they are. A subject submits a three-day diet diary, and the computer gives an energy analysis and compares the diet's nutrients to the Recommended Daily Allowances. Aaron believes a three-day diary is sufficient, since it has been found that people vary only slightly in their food habits, meaning they usually eat from the same basic food groups.

Below are the deficiencies Randi Aaron most commonly finds in women athletes whose diets are lacking. Some of the deficiencies can be caused by a simple lack of nutritional knowledge, but a high proportion of them are due to an alarming increase in the incidence of low body weight in active women. Such women are simply not eating enough. In fact, as a result of her research during a six-month study, Aaron believes that probably 1 in 10 women—a shockingly high number—is bulimic, which refers to the process of bingeing and then purging by self-induced vomiting or laxative and diuretic abuse in order to maintain weight.

1. *Anemia*—As detailed in the following chapter on iron, a good deal of the mineral is lost through heavy perspiration and menstruation. A good dose of iron from the diet is difficult to get, as at least 3,000 calories would be required to obtain it, and most women are not consuming this many calories overall—let alone in iron-rich food. Tiredness, paleness, and lack of energy are the symptoms of anemia, and in most cases iron tablets will solve the problem.

2. *Calcium*—Even sedentary women often don't get enough calcium, and it has been shown that increased exercise promotes calcium utilization. According to Aaron, even three cups of skim milk provide only the Minimum Daily Requirement of 800 milligrams. Therefore, an athlete should make sure to get an adequate amount of calcium, available in dairy products. Some of the best nondairy sources of calcium are sardines (from the bones), salmon, and green leafy vegetables.

3. *Folic acid*—An increased amount of folic acid is needed during exercise, and a deficiency is common among women. It is available in B-complex vitamins, green vegetables, beets, asparagus, broccoli, orange juice, legumes (peas and beans), and grains.

4. *Zinc*—The requirement for zinc also seems to increase with exercise. It is difficult to get in the diet, but is contained in greatest amounts in oysters, dairy products, brown rice and other grains, nuts—pecans, brazil, and cashews—and fish.

5. *Sodium and potassium*—Both sodium and potassium are lost through perspiration. However, a craving for salt actually signals the body's need for more water. Proper fluid replacement and a normal diet should alleviate the need for extra salt.

Potassium intake varies, and a deficiency may result in muscle cramps. Foods rich in potassium include mangoes (the highest fruit source of all, with double the amount of bananas), bananas, cantaloupe, oranges, apricots, dried fruits, nuts, flounder, halibut, cod, yams, lima beans, spinach, winter squash, avocadoes, potatoes, and broccoli.

The symptoms of exercise-induced hypoglycemia are fatigue and weakness or headache midway through exercise. Morning exercisers who like to run before eating may have this problem, caused by low blood sugar. The second type of exercise-induced hypoglycemia results in weakness or light-headedness during running, and may be caused by eating sweets fifteen or twenty minutes before a workout.

Two schools of thought exist on the subject of supplements, says Aaron. One is that a balanced diet contains all the necessary nutrients. Another is that supplements are often necessary and seem to improve performance. She feels it's unfortunate that no vitamin and mineral standards have yet been set for athletes, so the minimum or recommended amounts fail to take into account physical activity. And no one eats a normal diet 7 days a week, 365 days a year, she adds, so obviously one can't always get all needed nutrients. Because food intake may vary, and an athlete's requirements may be different, Aaron sees no detriment in taking supplements like B complex or Vitamin C—especially, she says, for runners, who tend to have certain poor food habits, like eating little during the day as it interferes with running or work, and making up for it with large amounts of food at night.

The most important principle for the athlete to understand is the proper ratio of protein/carbohydrates/fats in the diet. The diet for a distance runner should be comprised of about 65 percent carbohydrates—complex carbohydrates are recommended, such as whole grains, vegetables, and fruits—12 percent protein, and the remainder in fats. Randi Aaron sees a lot of athletes because they're more interested in nutrition than most, and because diet is so important for them. Of everyone in general she says, "When people start not feeling well, then they take an interest in their bodies."

17

Iron

WOMEN HAVE VARIOUS special nutritional needs even if they are not runners. Running emphasizes these needs, however, as it requires more stamina and a highly tuned body. The longer and harder you train, the more you become attuned to your level of strength and fitness. You notice small changes—when you feel especially good, or when you are tired, or even slightly off. Although women have the same physical response to training as men, some of their needs are different. One of them is the need for more iron due to menstrual bleeding or even heavy perspiration, and the increased possibility of iron deficiency, or even anemia.

From joggers to top runners, a number of women have problems with iron and anemia. Even the most experienced runners one would think have the best possible guidance have been plagued by iron deficiency—record holders Joan Benoit and Patti Catalano among them. Grete Waitz has said she takes iron every day, and says most of the women athletes in Norway do. Several top coaches report that iron deficiency is prevalent in many of their women runners, and evidenced in fatigue and decreased level of performance.

There are three basic stages of iron deficiency: iron depletion, iron deficiency without anemia, and iron deficiency anemia. It is important to realize that one can have any level of deficiency and still be affected in training, without having anemia itself. In fact, anemia is rare in women, but some degree of iron deficiency is fairly common. In a study of runners, some degree of iron deficiency was found in 55.6 percent.

Athletes and nonathletes are equally susceptible to iron deficiency, present in 25 percent of all menstruating women. However, an athlete will obviously notice it more, as the demand she places on her body is higher. Some studies have confirmed that vigorous exercise is associated with a higher demand for iron. An anemic person may feel more fatigue, experience a higher heart rate while running, and a longer recovery time after a workout. As women using an IUD may lose more blood during menstruation, they should be particularly careful to make sure they have enough iron.

On the other hand, some runners test anemic, but actually have a case of pseudoanemia or "runner's anemia." Despite low hematocrit or hemoglobin often found in their blood, it may be a sign that the body has produced expanded blood volume as an adaptation to training, which affects the results of this testing. It is important in this case, as in every incidence which is a result of, or affects your athletic life, to acquire the counsel of a doctor who is sensitive to the needs and problems of athletes, or works in the area of sports medicine.

Iron in the diet is critical for prevention of iron deficiency or anemia, and for the maintenance of strength. It is important in taking iron supplements, or eating iron-rich food, to understand the nature of absorption. Only about 10 percent of the iron ingested in the diet is absorbed. As a runner's food often passes quickly through the intestines, possibly even less iron is absorbed. It is best to maximize iron absorption, whether from food or in a supplement, by being aware of the following conditions. Iron is best absorbed on an empty stomach, so if you are taking iron supplements, try to do so a half hour to an hour before a meal. Absorption is enhanced by ascorbic acid (vitamin C) and also by meat, poultry, and fish protein. In addition, the iron from meat is better absorbed than that in vegetable sources. The use of iron cookware can increase iron content by five times.

On the other hand, protein from milk, cheese, and eggs, and tea and coffee can decrease iron absorption up to 80 percent. So can fat content in the diet, which is said to be very high in athletes' diets in both Europe and the United States. Although extra iron will pass out of the body, more is not better. The maximal safe tolerance level of iron such as ferrous sulfate has been shown to be 250 to 300 milligrams a day. Dr. Shangold claims that two or three iron tablets of this dose per week will provide all the needed iron, even for vegetarians or those with heavy periods. For iron-related problems, however, the dose of supplements should be based on a doctor's recommendation.

Another theory is that "runner's anemia" may be caused by the destruction of red blood cells from the trauma of repeated heel strike during running. In a study done by doctors in conjunction with the Nike Sport Research Laboratory, it was found that well-cushioned running shoes lessen the hemolysis caused by foot strike. Based on the results of this study, it is also recommended that one increase the intensity of running gradually to allow the body to adapt to the stress of training and to create new blood cells.

18

Anabolic Steroids

ANABOLIC STEROIDS are a synthetic form of male hormone, called androgens, which are taken in the belief that they increase strength and endurance. Athletes began to take anabolic steroids in the early 1950s in order to reduce muscle atrophy from disuse due to surgery. Their use grew in the 1960s when it was discovered that they produced additional beneficial effects for sports.

Anabolic steroids have traditionally been used by weight lifters and body builders. In track and field, they are mainly used by athletes who compete in events requiring explosive speed and strength, such as shot putting and discus throwing. It is believed that they build muscle strength and size, increase oxygen uptake (VO_2 max) and red blood cell count, and provide the ability to take on greater training loads due to faster recovery time. Since there is no conclusive scientific proof of physical benefits from anabolic steroids, the perceived benefits of their use is often attributed to a placebo effect.

Recently there has been speculation of anabolic steroid use among women distance runners, and it is predicted this use may grow. An increasing number of those in the running community, both coaches and athletes, are acknowledging that American women are experimenting with anabolic steroids, a practice that has been noted in Eastern European women. Since anabolic steroids increase strength characteristics associated with males, one coach points out why it is logical women would try the drug. "Most sports were originally designed for men, so obviously it is to a woman's advantage to have more masculine abilities." He adds, "Runners believe anabolic steroids allow them to do in a year what they would ordinarily do in four." Obviously a woman runner does not want the same effect from anabolic steroids as a shot putter, so each athlete, depending on his or her event, takes steroids in different doses and different cycles.

In 1979, the International Amateur Athletic Federation (IAAF) announced a discovery which shocked the athletic world. Seven East European women track and field athletes, among them three prominent middle-distance runners, had been banned from international competition for positive drug testing for anabolic steroids. "These are not the only girls who are not clean," said Grete Waitz of the banned women runners, who were her competition at the time. "This is one of the reasons why I wasn't interested in the Olympics. You know Russia and other East European countries will do anything to win the gold medal. The only thing I can do is train and run."

A position statement by the American College of Sports Medicine states that anabolic steroids may be harmful on a long-term basis, affecting reproductive function. Side effects of anabolic steroid use include menstrual irregularities, masculinization, increased body hair, acne, and possible enlargement of the clitoris. For these reasons, the college advises against the use of anabolic steroids by women.

But others caution against overstating potential risks when little is really known about anabolic steroids. One doctor has suggested that they may be as relatively benign as birth control pills. The conclusion of another expert is that in order to maintain their credibility, doctors should admit to athletes that little is known about steroids, rather than overstating the risks in an effort to deter athletes from taking them.

There may be debate over whether anabolic steroids enhance performance or cause detrimental side effects, but one thing is certain: they are illegal in international competition. They are part of a long list of performance-enhancing drugs containing banned substances. Testing for anabolic steroids is conducted in international competition, notably the Olympic Games, and is conducted via urine samples. Anabolic steroids raise questions about the possible risk of side effects and about the ethics of taking a drug that may improve performance. With sophisticated new systems of testing, there is a strong risk of disqualification from the Olympic Games.

19

Compulsion and Anorexia

Can Too Much of a Good Thing
Get Us into Trouble?

WHILE TRAVELING through the lush, expansive game parks of Africa in 1977, I began to feel an increasing anxiety over my imprisonment in a car. The animals were splendid, and I admired their speed and graceful movement, but why was I trapped behind a window, staring at them? It occurred to me that it was absurd to be so far removed from what they were doing: running around.

Running had become just as natural for me as it was for those animals. I did it because it felt as if I always had, and always would. But unable to run myself (even walking through the game parks is not allowed), I was forced to wait until my return to Nairobi, when I made a beeline for a swimming pool. I swam lap after lap, pausing only to perform the odd gesture of squeezing the sides of the pool—a physical reaction expressing my relief at finally being able to work out. Yet despite my relief, I was shocked at my dependence. I realized I had become hooked on exercise.

It was during this period that my weight, hovering at an all-time low of 110 pounds, dropped to 108 (I am 5 feet 6½ inches) and my clothing was taken in to a size 4. I worked out at least two hours a day, and I ate—when I felt hungry, that is. But I had disciplined most of my hunger away as I became more and more fascinated by watching myself grow slimmer and, I believed, stronger. It didn't represent vanity as much as it did challenge, discipline, and a clearer sense of self. Like tall, short, or blue-eyed, thin was the way I had become defined; it was what stood out about me, what people noticed. "You're so thin!" everyone would say, and my appetite would disappear as confirmation of this definition of myself. In a world of overweight people, I had control over my body. I was the healthy one. I was a winner.

Yet I suspect that something wasn't right about my instincts: curbing my appetite with carrot sticks, rinsing butter or oil from my food, and making sure not to go to bed on a "full stomach." I didn't feel unhappy, hungry, or without strength; I was just careful. I liked my thinner self and my eating habits, which were far from starvation, but spare enough to give me a sense of asceticism. Even if I were physically longing for food to gain the weight back, I never felt it. Something far deeper than my own conscious effort was controlling my appetite. It wasn't self-loathing; it was part of my desire to be a disciplined athlete.

Today at 118 pounds and a size 7, I am not as extreme about my regime, but I still eat carefully by average standards and feel the same motivation to maintain control of my body. Yet although I may have had anorexic tendencies, I know I didn't suffer from anorexia nervosa, nor have I ever, at least knowingly, behaved self-destructively toward my body, or wanted to.

Anne Snow* doesn't feel good without at least two hours of exercise a day. In college, where she was an outstanding cross-country runner, she ran 90 miles a week, never missed one of her double training sessions, and at 5 feet 7 inches weighed 103 pounds. Today at age 23, she claims she has "outgrown" the need for her strict college regime. Now she only runs an average of 75 miles a week, swims 2 to 5 miles a week, and weighs 109 pounds. She says she feels much more relaxed. She admits she is still compulsive, but claims she has never been anorexic. Her diet is mostly fruits and vegetables, and contains nothing with white sugar. Her daily intake of calories, almost all of which are consumed in one evening meal, is probably not much more than that of a sedentary woman. Says Anne, "I've always had a concern for staying thin, but I never starved or ate so little as to feel bad, weak, or sick." Although she vehemently denies it, most people say she is too thin, and categorize her as an anorexic.

Is Anne Snow lying to herself? And as my weight steadily dropped from 123 to 108 pounds, was I lying to myself about why? Although on different levels of intensity, does our behavior in fact constitute if not anorexia nervosa, then at least its main symptom: an unhealthy obsession with being thin? And what about the women more extreme than Anne, or the young girls just beginning to run who feel that initial interest with slimness? What is the difference between extreme compulsion and anorexia, and a healthy discipline and sense of purpose?

*Not her real name.

A growing number of women distance runners are particularly susceptible to the problem of anorexia in any of its stages. A woman runner's feelings of power, pride, and control—discussed earlier as positive attributes—are the same qualities that when carried to an extreme can develop into a dangerous obsession.

There is no denying that the feeling of running featherweight is powerful and intoxicating, and it is achieved as a result of the discipline and control of being a trained athlete. It isn't just a psychological high, either. Biological studies indicate that both anorexia and long-distance running can result in an increase in circulating endorphins, believed to affect both mood and pain.

In addition to thinness for speed, a woman runner's body is connected to her physical image much in the way that every woman's body has always been more in focus than a man's. Women runners belong to the same population of all American women, 95 percent of whom have been on a diet at one time or another. Yet a top male runner testifies that in eleven years of high school, college, and overseas running, he has *never* met a serious male runner who expressed special concern about his weight.

Anorexia nervosa, a disease afflicting mostly young, affluent girls, involves an extraordinary obsession with dieting and thinness, originating from a fear of becoming obese. This fear is not alleviated by weight loss, which represents at least 25 percent of original body weight. Estimates are that 100,000 to 150,000 women in the United States and Canada suffer from anorexia, and that 1 in every 300 women is anorexic.

Many of the women at any level of low weight tend to experience amenorrhea. Whether serious runner, compulsive runner, or anorexic, almost without a single exception every one of these women is amenorrheic at one time or another. Most women runners who don't get periods seem glad not to have them, and believe that it simply means their bodies are properly "shut off" during a time they are not meant to sustain another life through pregnancy.

Psychological motivations of anorexia include an effort to gain control in life represented by gaining control of the body, and avoiding physical development in fear of adulthood, sexuality, and childbearing. In personality type the anorexic is usually shy, with a shaky sense of self, and strongly achievement-oriented. Undeniably, the highly touted image of thinness as a sign of beauty and prestige contributes to the incidence of the disease. For the woman runner, thinness is a mark of status not only because it's fashionable, but because it's an external indication of athletic ability: the thinner, the faster.

Anorexia nervosa as a disease should not be confused with the word "anorexia," which simply means without appetite, and a condition that often happens with hard training. In addition, the anorexic, one suffering from the disease in which the primary objective is extreme weight loss, must be differentiated from the thin woman athlete, who may or may not suffer from anorexic tendencies, but who possesses an entirely different motivation for her behavior. Although they may seem, and may even eventually become the same person, they are separated by very basic differences.

"Anorexia nervosa entails the denial of biology," writes Sheila MacLeod in her insightful account of her anorexic girlhood, in which she talks of starving herself to 80 pounds to get closer to her skeleton, and thus to what she felt was the "real me." For an anorexic like MacLeod, being thin was an end in itself, a definition of self. This is not so for the woman runner, who genuinely believes being thin is a means to an end—running fast. And far from denying her biology, she is inextricably bound to it as a vehicle of her sport.

"Susan" was just this kind of runner, and her conclusion that "the thinner the better" led her to drop 30 pounds as a high school junior, at which time she was running 75 miles a week. From an ideal running weight of 112 (at 5 feet 4½ inches), Susan fell to a mere 78 pounds. Her initial weight loss, which at first coincided with her faster running, began to undermine her progress, until the all-American runner struggled through a mile race in 6:18.

Susan's is a classic case of the young runner who gets a warning from coaches and peers. "Watch your weight," her team was told. "This is a bad time to put on weight, when young girls change." After being hospitalized for a month and receiving counseling, Susan claims she realized the weight loss wouldn't make her run better, and that "it looked sick." Today she is 22 years old, still runs competitively, and claims she is cured. Her weight is 95 pounds.

Parents and coaches must constantly be on the lookout for anorexic athletes, and be careful to see the warning signs. "Some girls who run are too thin: I would call them 'subanorexics,'" says Dr. Peter Jokl of Yale-New Haven Hospital. Coach Brooks Johnson of Stanford University cites the disease as a major problem—as he astutely says, "especially the repressed anorexic, the one in the closet who will be gone before God gets the news." Johnson, who also believes "nonnutrition" has become a major cause of injury in runners, has the counsel of a nutritionist available for his athletes.

If "anorexic" and "cured" seem vague terms subject to individual definition, one thing is certain—the subject is on everyone's mind. "Anorexia" is today's fashionable word, and the first one often heard about a thin woman runner. Anne Snow makes a case against those who automatically accuse her, and others like her, of being anorexic. "What most thin female athletes are doing is trying to improve competitive ability in order to win. Part of winning is being different from everybody else—everybody is not a winner, a champion, an elite runner." When asked about her seemingly abnormal eating and training habits she answers, "What is normal? It's what is defined by people who aren't striving for the same things as the woman who wants to be an elite runner.

"An elite athlete has to pay more attention to the body. It's the body that she takes with her, that runs eighty miles a week, does speed work, and takes her through the race. It's her instrument. A thin, well-trained athlete may look different from everyone else because she *is* different than everyone else, but it's not a negative difference."

Being thin is a fact of life for a woman runner. Grete Waitz and Mary Decker, two of the world's best and not coincidentally slimmest distance runners, look the way they do for a reason, and they run fast partly for the same reason. Their slimness is a sign of speed, and a result of running hard and fast year after year. They are role models who are admired for their ability and success, as well as for their bodies, which are the vehicles of their achievements.

Concurring with the experts on anorexia, 27-year-old Gabriella VanderFluit of New Zealand says most anorexics cleverly deceive themselves as well as others by expounding an elaborate rationale when accused of having the disease. Gabriella's experience with anorexia at 16 (her weight plummeted to 85 pounds in six months) led her to give talks on the subject to groups of young girls.

She didn't consider herself anorexic at first, but now admits she started running to burn off more weight. Of her class of thirty girls, six suffered from the condition, a remarkably high 20 percent. "It occurs mostly during puberty," she says. "For a boy, there's bravado attached to becoming a man, but there is no bravado to becoming a woman, to gaining weight and getting a period."

If most women athletes are not exactly anorexics, whose obsession with thinness and starvation is a painful cry for help, many do share the same potentially dangerous characteristics. One of them is the obsessive-compulsive personality. Yet Anne Snow justifies her compulsion. "To be a champion athlete you have to be obsessed, directed toward achieving excellence. But it's okay, it's not like the obsession for an anorexic, which is dark and negative."

Maybe she's right. After all, compulsion in athletics is a passion, like any passion experienced by a person seeking ultimate achievement. The passion of an athlete is comparable to that of an artist, which seems so much more easily understood by society. The hands of the pianist are just as precious and fussed over as Anne Snow's body. Perhaps the woman runner's compulsion is simply the vehicle by which she seeks excellence.

Compulsion in artists or even men who aspire to Olympic gold medals is not disturbing, it's admired. Alberto Salazar's intense training is characterized as courageous, and no one ever called him sick or crazy for running 140 miles a week, or racing through serious bouts of dehydration, one almost fatal. But a woman who trains on a comparably intense level is believed to be living dangerously.

Why is the desire for excellence in a woman still considered suspect? "Running—An Analogue of Anorexia," a *New England Journal of Medicine* article points out, "When dieting or physical activity becomes an intense and exclusive focus, the woman tends to be categorized an anorexic, which connotes sickness, whereas the man will be viewed as an unusually dedicated athlete."

Is being thin just a part of the desire for excellence, or is it in fact part of a need to escape the demands of adult life? If running is partly play, and does in turn sustain childhood, is the woman runner's desire to be thin actually a desire to retain a child's body and her childhood with it? Is her battle to keep weight off merely a battle she is waging against her female biology?

"I thought you were a guy," said a male runner I passed on the road. Contrary to feeling insulted, I felt an almost naughty rush of joy for having "passed" as a man. I was happy for the absence of female flesh that shakes while running, and for the unobvious breasts and curves which aided me in my disguise. It wasn't that I wished I weren't a woman, but rather I was glad to be more like a man, who runs faster and looks better doing it.

According to studies, young girls express greater preference for the masculine role in American society because of its attributes of power and reward. "By getting thin, the successful woman adopts an adolescent boyish figure," says therapist Susan Waldman. "The feminine image doesn't quite fit in with her notions of competing and achieving, but the masculine image isn't right either. It's too threatening. This new figure falls somewhere in between." It may not be particularly healthy to admit identifying with wanting to be like a man, but the feeling exists, and I believe it does for many women runners, as well as for those women aspiring to excessive thinness.

The *New England Journal of Medicine* article on running and anorexia likenes "obligatory runners" and anorexic girls. It cited such common characteristics as gaining a sense of identity, autonomy, bodily control, "grim asceticism," and high achievement. The article claims that because both groups suffer an unsure sense of themselves, they seek to attain a better self-image through their respective activities. Although the article concludes that few runners or dieters become obligatory runners or anorexics, it states that at least 24 percent of anorexic women are intensely athletic, leading one to believe that the line between the compulsive woman runner and the anorexic may be as thin as the bodies in question.

The comparisons and allegations of the article were vehemently denied by many people in the running world. I believe the main fallacy of its conclusions lies in the issue which this chapter tries to make clear:

1. The athlete seeks to become the elite among runners, while the anorexic is the elite among dieters.

2. Although the compulsive runner and the anorexic share the same quest for perfection, one is clearly self-destructive, while the aim of the athlete is self-constructive. Despite the outcome for those who may be led to destructive behavior by overdoing their running and dieting, an important factor is their intention, which is not to achieve satisfaction or identity solely via thinness. Even if Anne Snow, for example, is in a constant state of controlling her biology by negative means, it is not her conscious intention to harm herself. Her intention is to become the best and fastest runner she can, in the best way she knows how.

There is no denying that compulsion is dangerous. It ignores the dictates of common sense and creates the possibility of self-destructive behavior. On the other hand, this same compulsion can be one of the necessary qualities of high achievement, and even of greatness. Beyond even devotion, excellence requires an endless drive and single-mindedness.

There are women runners who are anorexic. A *New York Times* article quotes health care professionals who have found an increasing number of their anorexic patients to be athletes. But anorexia is caused by a far deeper disorder in life than just getting carried away with becoming thin in order to run fast.

Dr. Claude Morias of Florida, who treated top North Carolina State runner Sue Overbey during her hospitalization for anorexia, claimed that "running is part of the blame." But in a long article on her dilemma, Overbey made no mention of running, yet spoke sincerely of the root causes of her disease. "There's no one thing I can put my finger on. It was everything. I began to lose control of my life—things I regret that I never faced earlier in my life. I should have dealt with them a long time ago but I blocked them out. I got really depressed and the severe depression brought on the weight loss. I just didn't want to eat."

Estelle Miller, director of the American Anorexia/Bulimia Association in New Jersey and a therapist who specializes in the treatment of the disease, agrees that the problem is much deeper than running. "It is caused by various factors, all of which must be determined by understanding the individual personality. One must ask, what does running represent? Why does the runner feel she needs to excel in this area?" Ms. Miller also points out an important social cause of the problem. "Women were suddenly told they could have it all—but no one told them how to get it."

The perplexing and relatively new dilemma of running and anorexia has yet to result in any clear answers, even from the experts. Meanwhile, it is only hoped that awareness, and if necessary therapy, may help the problem.

Certain revelations will ultimately separate the compulsive runner and the anorexic. While the disease can be fatal for the anorexic, long before this stage physical weakness will render a woman unable to run, and certainly unable to sustain the training load required to run fast. In fact, most serious women runners have at one time or another experimented with weight loss, and have discovered that under a certain weight there is a point of diminishing returns.

Another factor which may halt the problem is the realization that obsession with the body is never-ending, exhausting, and requires extreme regimentation. The energy a woman can use improving her running times is wasted when channeled to constant concern and anxiety over her body. Every athlete knows that one of the basic principles of successful running is relaxation, which is impossible when a woman has invested all her energy into a fanatic regime. Anne Snow admits that her college regime was so strict she had forgotten how to relax.

Thirdly, it is hoped that a woman may come to see that excessive obsession with the body is selfish and petty. After endless days of food-intake discussions (or lack of food-intake discussions), and watching slender women runners pinch their nonexistent fat in front of mirrors, it strikes one how shameful these concerns with extra bits of flesh are— preoccupations in a world that deserves more from us than angst over the size of our waist and thighs.

Those women who overcome their anorexia and learn to control their compulsion do so because something larger in life teaches them to see their sport in a new light. They realize it is not an ally in self-destruction or a vessel in which to pour personal frustrations. It is the privilege of the healthy and the living. It is meant to build, not to destroy.

20

How to Live With Injury

What to Do When
the Body's Answer Is "No!"

THERE IS NOTHING more distressing, yet more common, than injury or disability to an active runner (Who told us we were meant to pound our bodies into the ground thousands of times a day, anyway?); nor is there anything that seems to cause more physical and psychological anguish than those familiar withdrawal symptoms one suffers when rendered inactive. Your personality goes haywire; you're cranky; your hands shake—in short, you are literally and figuratively not yourself.

Being an active person in an active world is great when you're part of it, but not so great if you're disabled. It can be torture to watch friends and strangers running, or listen to the constant "jock's banter" of training and racing discussions. You feel left out not only physically, but socially. Learning to live with an injury sounds simple to the healthy, and to those who realize that in the realm of true life crises, not being able to run for a while ranks pretty low—like close to the bottom. It takes the wisdom of experience, however, to realize that tremendous change takes place within the body and mind of an active woman when she can't run. In fact, it can rock the foundation of her definition of self.

A layoff from running hits every athlete hard, but it seems that women have a greater difficulty dealing with the single most obvious consequence of curtailing their activity: weight gain. The truth is that women care about their weight. They're noticed more, and are usually more in tune with, and more dependent on, their bodies. While a man may understand athletic layoff—even from a distant memory of an old high school football injury—most women are learning to live with its consequences for the first time.

The key to successful running is learning how to prevent injury in the first place. Most elite runners have learned from years of experience how to monitor their bodies, listen to warning signals, take it easy when they need to, and build up their body's ability to handle the physical stress of running. Elite runners have been shown to associate with the body, that is, to constantly monitor its signals and be aware of its changes. It's the novice or less serious runner who has been shown to disassociate, separating the thought process from the body functions in order to escape discomfort. This is the runner who will recite poetry and recall childhood memories in order to get through a marathon, who will claim to have experienced "runner's high," while the elite runner will stay tuned to every body part for the entire 26.2 miles of the race.

The experienced runner learns the difference between the courage to push and running through the pain which is serving as a warning signal. Pain, fatigue, inability to sleep, depressed appetite, a higher than normal resting pulse rate, general apathy—these are all symptoms of overtraining, the primary cause of injury. The advice of all the best coaches is "Train, don't strain," and when it comes to considering your body, it can also be adapted to read "Use, don't abuse." The most important aspect of successful running is to learn to monitor the body—to be with it, not removed from it. When you learn to read its signals, you can help prevent injury before it sidelines you.

However, some injury is probably inevitable for most of us. It is no small task we undertake when we put our bodies through mile after mile of pounding on unsympathetic concrete, and no small request we make to ask the body to hold up unscathed under it all. If an injury doesn't heal with slow jogging or a layoff, and self-help steps like buying new shoes or icing a sore spot don't work, it's probably time to consult a doctor.

There are now enough doctors and other specialists who deal in running injuries for you to be able to find one who understands yours, and understands you. Don't settle for the unsympathetic type who says you shouldn't run so much, or at all, or who doesn't have experience treating runners. Word of mouth is a good way to find a specialist, but if all your friends are healthy and you don't know one, look up a sports medicine center at a major hospital, or check the Resource List in the back of this book for help.

What do you do when you can't run? Well, you need not relinquish your fitness by sitting and waiting for the injury to heal. There are alternatives, depending on what ails you. Here are some possibilities:

Swimming or Biking   Both of these activities are often used as a supplement to running as well as a substitute, as they provide an additional workout without adding the stress of pounding the legs. If you're not a great swimmer, try running in a pool. Merely perform the same running movement while standing upright in the water. Actually, "merely" is not the right word; it's plenty difficult, but at least you don't have to be a good swimmer. Grete Waitz admits she's no fish in the water, and has tried this method while injured. The resistance provides plenty of a workout. If you don't have a bike, or it's too cold outside, try buying or borrowing a stationary bike or using one at a Y or a health club. Practice pedaling at different resistances, or harder and faster at intervals, as you would with running.

Weight Lifting   No matter which system you use—Universal, Nautilus, or free weights—you can either begin or increase weight work while you're not running. Not only does using weights improve general muscle tone, but it helps strengthen muscles left weak by inactivity, particularly those muscles which support the area of injury. It is not only a good substitute activity, but good for rehabilitation as well. This may prove essential to your comeback, and as a preventive measure for the future.

If weight facilities are unavailable, inexpensive dumbbells or ankle weights can be used at home, or even shoulder bags filled with books, which can be used for leg lifts. Toe lifts on stairs or books strengthen the calves. The important point is, when without, improvise! Get a book of weight exercises for guidance; lift anything that's around; walk when you used to ride; take the stairs.

Now is an opportunity to see if you would enjoy adding alternative forms of exercise to your running. Consider what marathon world-record holder Joan Benoit had to say when she took up alternative training methods after injury. "Bicycling, swimming and weight training have now replaced the excessive mileage that served no constructive purpose. These other activities have allowed me to enjoy running more than ever, since I am refreshed and eager when I do step on the roads. I feel now that my body is more balanced and synchronized and as a result I am running more efficiently."

Home Remedies   Get a comprehensive book on running injury and employ methods like ice therapy or aspirin. For sore muscles or muscles stiff from injury, I have discovered plastic wrap, especially at night while sleeping to avoid morning stiffness. Wrapping in plastic keeps the heat in and acts as a "mini sauna," keeping muscles loose. You can even wrap your waist for back stiffness. It may sound a bit kinky, but it works miracles!

Eating Raw Vegetables That's right, this and other methods to curb your appetite are the disabled runner's answer to gaining weight. Nothing will dampen your mental outlook more, or make it harder to get back in shape, than putting on extra pounds, and the stress of added weight doesn't help an injury, either. Instead of all the unlimited helpings you allowed yourself during training, use dieters' tricks. Try eating raw carrots or celery. It really does help to chew yourself to the end of dinner, and by the time you finish, the meal is over anyway! If you feel a hunger that running helped suppress and you want to be careful to control it, start by eating the most "innocent" foods first. Have a high-protein snack and give it at least twenty minutes—that's how long it takes the "hunger center" in the brain to get the message you've eaten. You'll find you may be satisfied with less than you thought you needed. Use the layoff time to take on the challenge of a new and better diet, rather than deciding you'll run off extra pounds when you heal. Diet has a tremendous psychological impact, and the latter tack will only make you feel worse.

Reading, Writing, and Other Intellectual and Cultural Pursuits You know, those activities you used to do before all that running rendered you too tired to lift your arms, let alone if they were holding a book. This is a good opportunity to use the time and energy you usually devote to running to do the many other activities that have suffered neglect since they became second priorities.

Philosophy If you're an exercise addict, it's a good time to put life in perspective. All the cures in the world can't replace the wisdom and understanding you gain after a forced layoff. Now maybe you can fully appreciate the importance of running to you, and besides, your life as an athlete won't end because you can't run for a while. Remember that it's a lifestyle choice above all else, and yours to live with as long as you choose.

I once asked top runner Katie MacDonald what best seemed to help her career-long back problem. Expecting answers like chiropractics or whirlpools, or even "I run right through it," she instead gave a most sobering answer. "Patience," she said with the smile of a Buddha. There's no magic cure or doctor who can do what time can.

I once asked Matt Centrowitz, Olympian and coach, what special methods of training he uses with his successful runners. He said it's easy to train distance runners, as they are all highly motivated, and added, "It's common sense. When you're tired, or you don't feel well, you simply don't run." Simple advice, but from someone who should know.

You'll never realize how much a part of your life running has become until you don't have it. And there's nothing you can do to prepare yourself for the realization, or the mental and physical difficulty of being without it.

Sometimes contemplating all the misery in the universe won't calm the floods of panic that invade me when I can't be the athlete I've always been. Yet when I've been laid off, I try to keep it in perspective, and remember that in the scope of the world's problems, mine are absurdly minute.

Life does go on, and healing almost always comes in time. There will be that moment when you do run again, as if there had been no pain, no injury. The best thing about that first run will be the freshness of it, and the joy and freedom you feel from being well. But more, injury and recovery will have given you the ability to remember, and to appreciate.

Part III
Running and Winning

21

Competition

WHEN GRETE WAITZ pulled away from her competitors and took the lead in the first World Championships marathon, television commentator and Olympic marathon winner Frank Shorter observed, "She has made her commitment." Grete had taken those decisive strides that announced she intended to take the lead and keep it. She was making it clear to herself, and to the other women in the race.

When we undertake a running program, no matter what our goals, we make the same commitment. We announce that we are undertaking a quest for self-improvement and a lifestyle that is symbolized by health and strength. But the commitment goes even further when we enter the world of competition.

Running offers competition for all levels and all ages. And contrary to the idea that the "fitness fad" is merely an attempt to prolong or capture youth, running celebrates achievement regardless of age, and in fact, often because of it. When 81-year-old Ruth Rothfarb ran the New York City Marathon in 1981, she received almost as much attention and cheering as the winners. Races offer women the opportunity to test themselves in new ways, and to share their experiences with others. And it is never too early to start, or too late.

Many organizations and sponsors conduct all-women's races and have developed separate systems of timing, scoring, and awards for women in mixed races. The New York Road Runners Club, which conducts the L'eggs Mini Marathon with over 6,500 women, established a model for a separate women's finish line in mixed races, and has lobbied for equal media coverage for women's events, with particular success on network television in the 5th Avenue Mile and the New York City Marathon.

Most women were not born into an atmosphere in which they learned to identify with sports, not even passively as fans. So television exposure of women's races offers new possibilities to find role models. And when women discover for themselves the emotions which arise from athletic competition, life can change dramatically. Becoming a runner, and then a competitor, often leads a woman to feel as if an entire new world is being revealed to her. She is right.

It is the world of exploring one's limits. It is a model for other challenges in life, expressed by such running terms as "putting it on the line," "getting a second wind," "crossing the pain threshold," "going for it." And what is learned in a race is applied to other endeavors in life, other challenges and goals.

The race is a model for life, but significantly, *active* life, not passivity. Nothing is achieved by watching from the sidelines, and no one can run for someone else. Racing celebrates what all women strive for: pride and independence, because when the starting horn sounds, each woman as an individual must make it to the finish for her own victory. She must call up her own reserves and experience to make her journey. It is an exercise of a newfound power for a woman, the power that derives from realizing her own determination and potential.

Racing allows one to set attainable goals. Mary Gilbert, public relations manager for L'eggs, sponsor of the 10-kilometer women's Mini Marathon, makes this point. "The fact that in two hours or less, sixty-five hundred women have accomplished what they set out to do is an achievement of great immediacy. You just don't see that on such a large scale in other areas in life. Careers, relationships—these things take time."

The aggressive nature of sports competition has often been used as an excuse for women's lack of involvement in sports, and for illustrating the negative aspects of competition in our society. Competition traditionally fosters the idea that, as famous football coach Vince Lombardi said, "Winning isn't everything; it's the only thing."

Despite incredulous journalists who wondered why Grete Waitz wasn't more upset at losing her first of five races in the 1983 L'eggs Mini Marathon, Waitz told them she was happy just to finish second. Her race, run at less than 100 percent effort due to illness, indicated to her how good her overall conditioning really was.

The following day's edition of the *New York Times* featured a picture of

Waitz and winner Anne Audain embracing at the finish line. Redefinition of the competitive ethic is clearly possible when one considers the point made by pioneer feminist Betty Friedan. Until now the term "achievement," as well as other social values, has been "defined by men and measured in terms of male experience." In fact, studies suggest that the "fair play" ethic is more frequently found in females than males.

Perhaps women can transcend the negative aspects of athletic competition. Perhaps they can instill it with a new humanity and teach both men and women the grace of losing as well as winning, an attitude of dignity despite performance—and just good sportspersonship!

Once in the competitive situation, whether out to beat the clock or a runner up ahead, a woman has the chance to test herself in new and unique ways. She discovers how much she wants to achieve a goal, what she is willing to endure to reach it, and how she reacts to the mental and physical stress involved. From the second the starting signal sounds, the racer must be like a scientist, carefully monitoring and analyzing not only herself but those around her. Am I breathing hard? Am I tired? How is the woman next to me feeling, or the one ahead?

Racing is an art which requires frequent and constant practice. As former world class runner Marty Liquori has written, "Running and other endurance sports are the most unforgiving of mistresses. You can drop out of law school for a year and come back to it later, picking up where you left off. Few things, certainly not knowledge, fade as quickly as the results of hard physical training. It is a flower that does not last long past the picking."

When the race is bad, it can be very difficult, yet few runners ever drop out of a race. For those who have undertaken the discipline of the training, running the race is an opportunity to carry something through. There are things in life in which we cannot last because we have little control over them, but runners, able to determine their own fate in a race, feel all the more determined not to quit. Despite how difficult racing can be, we do it again. We come back to it, because each time we race we learn something new about ourselves, and especially during those times when we test our personal limits and ability.

When Mary Decker gritted her teeth and sped ahead of her Russian competitors in the final meters to win two gold medals in the World Championships, millions of spectators cheered. Few sights have impressed so many, and told them so much about determination.

When the race is good, when all the training and hard work come together and you're floating almost effortlessly, you understand why you do it. You understand why it makes you feel strong and powerful, and why it is worth the training. You are your own person then, unique in your role on the stage of this great performance: the race.

To toe the starting line of a road race may make your knees rattle and your mouth turn dry. To be there is to acknowledge your fear of testing yourself and to accept that you will undergo the trial. When you do, you take on the toughest challenge: the one against yourself.

Too many women have for too long been afraid: afraid to venture, to risk, to somehow be exposed in what they judge a failing effort. But a race is a support system of thousands of people, providing an arena in which it is safe to take new risks. Runners realize that no matter what they feel in a race, they are not alone. Pain or fear, as well as joy, is part of the camaraderie of road races.

Unlike many fitness schemes, particularly those aimed at women, there's no claim that running is always fun and easy. On various levels, it is downright painful. It's work, and pushing the body hard or fast can hurt, but this is all the more reason why millions of people keep doing it. A runner's training is practice in overcoming pain and pushing beyond it in order to become strong. And if strength is learned through running, surely that same strength can be applied to other areas of life.

In everything important you do, you promise yourself to do your best. That is what it means to make a commitment to running, and to competition: to train, to race, to take the lead—in life as well as in running.

22

Women's Coaches

and the State of the Art in Distance Running

"Coaching is no different from what a choreographer does with a dance or what a playwright does with plays."

Brooks Johnson
Runner's World
January 1983

BEING COACHED is what turns running from a hobby into a vocation, a pastime into full-time. And a commitment to a coach and/or a team is what separates the joggers from the true believers. No matter what the level of a woman's ability, the minute she takes on the structure of coach and team—she's serious.

It wasn't so many years ago when a woman runner found, or more often was found by, a coach only by accident. Whereas "no man is an island"—male runners had teams and programs throughout school and after graduation—women had close to nothing at all. A woman runner *was* an island, floating without direction. According to a recent study by the Metropolitan Athletics Congress in New York, in 1970 there were fewer women's track and field programs in the entire country than there were for just boys' high schools in New York City!

Today the majority of colleges and universities have a women's track team, and of the fifteen hundred TAC (The Athletics Congress) teams in the United States, many of them include women. Women who once trained for distances no longer than 800 meters, and who did so only until college age at the latest, are now taking advantage of the new popularity of road races from one mile to the marathon and beyond, run by women of all ages.

Without exception, almost every top woman runner today benefits from the guidance of a coach. The coaching profession is becoming more and more advanced as distance running develops, techniques get more sophisticated, and races get more competitive. Coaching is an art—a bit like teaching, a little like counseling—and a coach is part friend, mentor, and adversary all in one. A successful coach/athlete relationship takes a tremendous amount of respect, trust, patience, and experience. Coaching is not an easy task. As Stanford coach Brooks Johnson says, "Just because you take a stopwatch and put a whistle in your mouth doesn't mean you're a coach."

What makes a woman runner good today, as opposed to ten years ago, is determined by an entirely new set of standards, reflected not only in race times but in both physical and psychological development. And while there are still legions of women with undiscovered talent, runners are beginning earlier and earlier to establish an athletic base. Every year in this country girls are breaking 50 percent of the high school track and field records, and their participation in athletic programs has soared over 500 percent.

Several trends seem characteristic of today's coaching. Some of them are related to the psychology of being an athlete, but as women become more used to competing, the main emphasis is on the training itself. In distance running, training intensity and speed are the name of the game.

While most coaches still employ a base of long slow distance (LSD), this technique is not the focus of training it used to be. When Bob Glover, coach of the Atalanta Track Club and co-author of the *Competitive Runner's Handbook,* started training women back in 1975, they did mostly distance workouts. He claims they weren't far enough along in their running to take on the physical stress of speed. As women became more used to the physical demands of running, they began to do speed work and interval training. But the key was, and still is, to make a woman an athlete first before introducing the rigors of speed work.

The focus of coach Tracy Sundlun's program is to make his adult women runners better athletes. This is a more comprehensive approach than he uses with his college-age athletes, those women who already have competitive backgrounds. "I just point the experienced runner in the right direction and her competitive background and instincts take care of the rest," says Sundlun, whose Warren Street Social & Athletic Club includes a handful of sub-2:40 women marathoners. Sundlun's other credentials in his lifelong involvement in coaching include stints with teams in several universities as well as postgraduate clubs, and as Olympic coach for the national teams of Puerto Rico and Antigua.

Sundlun's experience with runners affects his approach to coaching. "Most people have no concept they could be really good at something. I try to create expectations and the right environment for them to improve, and I set no limits on them."

Bob Glover, whose women's team has won the Avon International Marathon Championship title several times, provides the necessary support and confidence via heavy emphasis on the team concept. "We think of ourselves as a family," he says, and he adds that the object of the group is not just to run fast, but to be comfortable together and supportive of each other, creating a team feeling similar to that in a college or a high school.

But Brooks Johnson doesn't have to deal with the same issues as Glover and Sundlun. He has the competitive structure and group commonality already built into his Stanford University team. When Johnson, who has coached both men and women, is asked if women runners are any different psychologically or emotionally than men, his answer is right to the point: "bull———." In fact, Johnson believes women may be superior in certain respects such as higher pain threshold and a greater ability to undergo stress, because, as he believes, they are constitutionally suited to childbirth.

All three of these coaches maintain that their systems are not gender-oriented. They train athletes, and they do it no differently for women than for men. Bob Glover, however, does feel strongly about maintaining an all-women's group in his team's twice weekly workouts. He claims there is more positive stress when women run against each other, which gives them an advantage in all-women's races. Tracy Sundlun, however, whose team is coed, feels that what is important in workouts and races is for his athletes to relate to and train with any runner who has broken a certain barrier.

The key to the success of women's running today is speed, the techniques of which are adapted from track training. Johnson defines racing as "going from one point in time and space to another in the shortest elapsed time." He immediately adds, "What is precious and critical is speed. Endurance is not the problem." Sundlun's coaching objective is similar: "increase of flow speed"—which is the ability to prolong a rapid rate of leg turnover. Both employ techniques to develop sprinting ability and the fast-twitch muscle fibers,* which must be educated by constant use. Of sprint-

* See footnote on p. 53 for an explanation of fast and slow twitch fibers.

ing ability, Johnson cautions, "Use it or lose it." Glover's two speed sessions per week, constructed seasonally with varying intensity, are also based on the need to develop similar skills.

All three of these coaches are highly experienced and successful, but conduct slightly different programs. It is instructive to consider each of them.

Brooks Johnson is one of the most highly respected coaches in track and field. His qualifications are evident in the fact he was named the women's head coach for the 1984 Olympic team. In addition to his college team, which is one of the nation's top collegiate women's teams, Johnson has turned out a long list of all-Americans and national champions.

The Stanford women log an average of 50 to 60 miles a week, and run speed sessions once, twice, but no more than three times a week. The amount of speed work depends on the individual athlete and her lactic acid buildup (the cause of the stiff feeling in the legs that signals the need for rest). Johnson says the way to develop speed is by increasing stride length and rate. The point of his approach is to get the body used to rapid turnover. "If a runner uses sixty-five percent of maximum turnover in a race, the practice tempo must be thirty-five to forty percent higher than that figure. It is the same with the hundred meters or the marathon."

Bob Glover defines his system by its five phases:

- Endurance phase: during which his runners, who log an average of 50 to 90 miles a week, run only one speed workout a week, without being timed. They may run a few low-key races during this phase.
- Strength training phase: includes a lot of hill work, with the addition of a second speed workout, including some timed intervals. A few races may be run, fairly well but not sharp.
- Sharpening phase: in which two hard workouts a week include one on the track. During this phase, several good races are used to sharpen the athlete mentally and give her the chance to set personal best times. A race like a major marathon is a "big risk event," according to Glover, and several good races leading up to the main event salvage part of the training cycle in case something goes wrong in the big race.
- Tapering phase: allows the runner to cut back the mileage and rest.
- Rebuilding phase: brings the athlete back to one speed workout a week, not for time. The length of this phase depends on the length of the race. After a marathon, for example, it is 4 to 6 weeks.

Tracy Sundlun's Warren Street team includes about sixty women, some of whom live in different parts of the country or attend school during the year. Those in the New York area attend two organized practice sessions a week. Sundlun makes a significant point when asked about seasonable training. "I basically train road racers, and there is no road racing season. Pick any month or week and you can find an important road race." He says his athletes train year-round and improve year-round, and focus periodically on big races of their choice.

All Warren Street-ers do some form of speed work at least eleven months of the year. Two sessions a week are held one day apart and are structured as follows:

- Tuesday consists of longer, more endurance-oriented work. The time of the interval is more significant than the time of the rest, which is uncontrolled. The intervals are a half mile and longer.
- Thursday's intervals are shorter, a quarter mile and under, and emphasize the rest portion, or controlled rest. More sets of these intervals are run than of the longer variety.

Sundlun also brings to his coaching the sprint philosophy that Johnson employs, and includes techniques based on sprint drills. Each workout session consists of an extensive warm-up of resistance stretching, a mile of short pickups (picking up pace), high knee drills, and bounding and skipping drills. The theory behind these drills is to strengthen the muscles which distance running does not develop, as these are the areas which "go out" on the runner in a race or an overload situation. Another significant aspect is Sundlun's concern with form. Proper form is more economical, and increased stride length alone via the drills can cut minutes off a runner's time, he contends.

Warren Street runners may also attend kinetics classes, which teach body awareness and control. The purpose of the classes is to instill an understanding of how the body moves, an added advantage, says Sundlun, over the other women on the starting line, and especially important for those women who have not grown up with athletic backgrounds.

Each of these coaches, as well as all successful coaches, brings to his profession more than just technical know-how. Personality cannot be overlooked as being one of the greatest aspects of coaching success.

Brooks Johnson, a forceful and articulate man, comes across as blunt, yet with a great deal of wisdom and humanism. He describes his theory of coaching. "There's one prima donna, and that's me. This cuts out a lot of crap. A coach has to work from his or her own strength, and the fact is that I can scare people. When you step to the line in a race, there is fear—the ghost in the mind. So it's a trade-off: you fight the ghost, or me.''

But there really is little to fear in a race for Johnson's athletes. Says Johnson, ''We don't ever talk about winning; we talk about being successful, meeting one's own potential. The athlete is well prepared and well coached. Everything is broken down.''

Bob Glover relies heavily on the team concept, and believes that individuals improve due to team structure. Because he coaches women not in college, he emphasizes the difference in their needs, and tries to aid the athlete in ''balancing the athletic life with job, career, and family.'' Although there are ability requirements for joining Atalanta, Glover says, ''We want to be elite but not elitist.''

Although the work load is equally high for Tracy Sundlun's athletes as for other teams, he says his athletes are out to have a good time as well as run races. His club is known for its more lighthearted approach to running and racing.

All three coaches mention the need to hold their athletes back—keep them from overdoing it. ''Rest is an integral part of our program; you can't hammer all the time,'' says Brooks Johnson, who is faced with the problem of dealing with overachievers and overdoers—a Stanford way of life. Bob Glover notes that the new woman runner is hungrier than her predecessors, but without the strong athletic background her body is not ready for intense work loads. Tracy Sundlun claims, ''To be great you have to have the mentality to push yourself to extremes. A coach has to teach a person to be patient and reasonable.''

The obvious question of course arises: Why aren't there more *women* coaches of women runners? Tracy Sundlun gives several reasons. ''Sports in general have drawn few enough brains, and amateur sports even fewer brains. It used to be that a woman couldn't find a coach at all. With Title IX at least men accepted their presence. Then when a woman found a coach she followed him based on whether or not she liked him as a person, not on whether he was a good coach. She had no choice anyway.'' Brooks Johnson says there aren't that many coaches, period, and women are second-class citizens in athletics on top of it. Finally, Bob Glover adds that we will probably see more women coaches in five or ten years when the women who are now competing retire and devote time to coaching.

It's even worse than this, however. A December, 1983, study revealed that not only are women coaches not being hired, their numbers are decreasing. There are 437 more male head coaches in universities today than five years ago, a 13 percent increase. Female coaches number 249 fewer today than five years ago, a 209 percent decrease! This obviously isn't helped by the fact that women are also pitifully underrepresented in athletic administration. The study also revealed that 80 percent of intercollegiate sports programs have male department heads, while 30 percent of university programs are administered without any female representation at all.

The nature of the woman athlete/male coach relationship causes certain complications. First of all, one wonders what motivates a man to want to coach women. Both Brooks Johnson and Tracy Sundlun speak of coaching athletes, and deemphasize gender. But Bob Glover says he made the decision to coach women specifically when one of his first women runners came to him and said, "I want to be a good runner." Says Glover, "I looked into her eyes and saw something different." In addition to appreciating their drive and determination, obviously the coach of these new women athletes is going to experience added satisfaction at both their rapid improvement and the new status they are afforded.

So close is the woman athlete to her male coach that more than a few coach/athlete relationships end up in romantic partnerships or marriage. Sports psychologist Linda Lewis Griffith attributes this largely to the fact that these women feel understood by their coaches. "One of the biggest problems for women athletes is that they often feel alone. They're more likely to hear: 'Why run so much?' or 'Why not party more?' Other men don't seem to understand them as much as their coaches." Perhaps no one, man or woman, will ever know the athlete as intimately as her coach, and so it is understandable that she may become dependent on him for more than his advice on training and racing.

It is the guidance provided by good coaching, and the support of a team structure, that can make a good runner great. Coaching can help all women to enter the world of sports which has so long been closed to them, and can make a woman the best athlete she can be.

23

Conquering Fear

We have no reason to mistrust our world, for it is not against us. Has it terrors, they are our terrors; has it abysses, those abysses belong to us; are dangers at hand, we must try to love them.

"Letters to a Young Poet"
Rainer Maria Rilke

IT IS October 23, 1983, the day of one of the world's largest and most famous athletic events, the New York City Marathon. Today I will coanchor race-announcing on WABC Radio, which will be broadcast live to over one and a half million people. As I put the headphones on at the finish line in Central Park, the director makes a crisp slice with her hand, signaling that we are on the air. Suddenly it hits me that I must fill three hours with words, and there is absolutely no margin for error in what I say. Yet I feel as calm as a yogi on a mountaintop. I have been here before, and I am not afraid.

The rest of the year is different. It is a Saturday. It is a Sunday. It is any weekend, many weekends. I stand in a tightly bunched crowd of runners, watching cars and trucks being loaded with press people and officials. The red light on the lead truck is swirling. Some of the runners are chatting or laughing; others are nervously shaking their legs or arms. I see a few friends and a few familiar faces. I stand among thousands; no one is watching me. When the starting horn sounds, I will take off with thousands, and when I finish, I'll be one of thousands. My hands are cold and clammy; my knees are rumbling like the beginning of an earthquake; I have to go to the bathroom for the tenth time. Inside me looms a terror too great to imagine. I have been here before, and yet I am still afraid.

Hanna Sheziffi, veteran Israeli runner, multi-time Asian Games champion and Olympic competitor, once said that even after fifteen years of competitive running, she was still nervous. "Before every competition I swear I'll quit, because the tension almost drives me crazy, but I run, and afterwards I forget the feeling."

Thousands of women, and men for that matter, who stand ready to run the first race of their lives feel the same terror as the veterans. Thousands of people are afraid to run at all—afraid of the pain, the fear of being seen, or what others may think of them. Why are we frightened, and can we overcome the fear?

Whether we are beginning runners, or dream of becoming world-class competitors—we are all at some point faced with feelings of fear. Is it because some harm may come to us in a race, or we may somehow be exposed? (Our spare clothing of shorts and singlets makes the latter a literal truth.) Is it because we fear we may not complete what we set out to do, and may find ourselves "failures," or be judged that way by others?

The fear of the race is all of these fears. It is the fear of the unknown, and the feeling we are headed straight into it.

Just as sport teaches us about ourselves, and allows us to express vital instincts, so too may athletic endeavors frighten us. Because sport provides us with so many experiences and emotions, we must accept that fear is one of them.

Each time we stand on the starting line, we face the possibility that we will fail. It is the fear that grows from a gap in confidence, for we are in a realm which feels risky. Our success may be limited, and we take many chances in a sport that can provide satisfaction one day and defeat the next.

Yet when we do something we know well, have done many times, we are calm and confident. We know we are capable because we have the experience of success. Perhaps we are led to think, If only I could run a race with that same sure feeling! Maybe then we would have more days like those when we felt we were ready, when we believed it would "come together," and when we achieved our goal—be it a win, a personal best time, or just finishing.

When Alberto Salazar came to the New York City Marathon in 1981, he calmly told the press he intended to break the twelve-year-old marathon world record. Words like "brash" and "cocky" circulated the room. But Salazar merely spoke with undisguised confidence. "If they knew Alberto like I do," wrote his wife Molly two years later, "they would know he speaks straight from the heart." Salazar claimed that according to his training, he knew he was ready and that he could do it. And he did, coming across the line in 2:08:13.

The race is like a final exam. If you have prepared, you have nothing to fear. Marty Liquori, former world-ranking distance runner, has written that much of the pain in a race is due to fear. "The elite runner feels the same sensations as all other competitors, but he or she has learned to interpret them not as alarming signals that the body is self-destructing (he or she knows better from long experience), but as indications that the pace may be too fast, warning signs that lactic acid is too high, or that fuel reserves are low."

Each of us knows things in our life the way Salazar knew he could run that record. I know I can speak on the radio. I know it from experience. A mother of several children doesn't fear giving birth, because she's done it before. Business executives know they can close deals, pilots know they can fly, mountain climbers know they can make it to the top—all because they have done it before, or practiced doing it.

The beauty of racing is that it allows most of us to test ourselves in situations in which we will not be judged by others, in which we face no threat of "losing," yet which offer us a challenge each and every time we toe the starting line. And there is no perfection, no limit to aspiration. We can always run faster, or further. Even Alberto Salazar can break his own world record. "Why come back to New York," I once asked Grete Waitz, "when you have won the races so many times? What's left as a challenge?" "Another year, another marathon, is always a challenge to me," she answered.

It is encountering the fear, not avoiding it, that will make us strong and enable us to find fulfillment. This is why we continue: to try, to train, to race. As we did so many years ago when we learned to walk, to catch a ball, to make ourselves understood, we will continue to try, despite the fear we face. It is our nature.

There is only one way to conquer a fear, and that's by facing it—head on. In this respect we are the great adventurers of our time and of our own lives. We are not content to give up; we do not stop half-done, and we will be satisfied only when we have confronted and undergone the challenge.

In a society in which much of the challenge has been removed, in which our day-to-day survival is not questioned, we seek other ways of being tested. Because we need not hunt for food, travel great distances to survive, or fight wars to exist, we are guaranteed a certain ease in life. But ultimately it isn't enough. We are forever unfulfilled when we have not fulfilled ourselves.

America experienced a great social rebellion in the sixties and seventies after upper-middle-class parents had given their children "everything" in the fifties. After suffering the hardship of the war years, they believed that providing an easy and safe life was the greatest gift they could give their children. They were wrong. The young generation lived a life full of protests, and of risks. They challenged materialism, racial inequality, and the Vietnam war.

Leave people to their safety, their leisure, and they will seek the difficult, facing fear willingly. It is our nature to desire challenge, and this is what the race provides. This is part of what fitness is all about. The work, the sweat, the discomfort, the investment, and ultimately even the fear are the essential ingredients of the challenge we so willingly undertake.

Because many women have not been encouraged to take on challenge and face fear, these principles may be foreign at first. Women have always been taught to find outside support, to be guarded from challenge. There is still the impression that women aren't strong and able enough to endure the athletic life. So a woman must work harder, and overcome more, to feel comfortable in a world in which she initially feels herself to be a stranger.

Phyllis Friedman has done a lot in her 50 years. She has raised five children, three of whom have run competitively since high school. She has a successful teaching career to which she devotes almost all her energy. While she was raising the children and teaching school, there was never any question of doing anything for herself, she says. Going out for a run? It just wasn't done.

But today she finds herself a runner, and tries desperately to maintain her running routine. To do so, she realizes, she must redefine her priorities and change her lifestyle. It is second nature for her to raise children or to teach them, but to make time for a daily run is infinitely more difficult. Because she does not want to lose her newfound fitness, or her battle with her weight, Phyllis says of her running, "I'm afraid to stop."

What does it feel like to conquer the fear? "The first days I went out running, it felt awful. My chest hurt so badly. I was frightened." But three months later, and 20 pounds lighter, Phyllis Friedman adds, "Today I feel like I'm in control of myself. I feel good."

Yet no matter how many fears we conquer, more await us. The fear we feel on the starting line the first time is in many ways the same as the fear we feel the hundredth time—but it doesn't mean we won't go to that line again. No matter how many races we run, we may always be afraid at the start, and relieved when the race is over. We're not alone—even the top elite runners feel the same way.

Refusal to accept challenge is refusal to face fear, and we cheat ourselves when we turn away from challenge, when we don't enter the contest. Yet believing that to face fear once is enough is to be open to the terrible disappointment that results when one realizes that fear never leaves us. When we have overcome one hurdle, many others await us. At the finish line of every race is always the announcement of the next one.

When we run a race, we leave a comfortable world in order to face the unknown. There is no denying the fear; it is there to greet us whether we accept it or ignore it. In order to overcome the fear of racing, or even just stepping out the door to run, we must do these activities many times until we are comfortable with them, and until the unknown becomes known.

Through training and racing, we learn to understand what is happening to our bodies, what pain is telling us. It's not something we need fear, but rather a challenge to remain calm and gain understanding. One of the basic principles of running a race, or competing in any sport, is relaxation. As soon as the athlete is overcome by fear or anxiety, the legs tighten, the head drops back, the race is lost.

For some, conquering fear will simply mean stepping out the door and taking the first running steps. For Phyllis Friedman, it means going beyond her longest run of 5 miles. For others, it is toeing the starting line of a race, or running a marathon, setting a pace that promises a personal best, or taking the lead for a win.

"When a woman says to herself, 'I could never run twenty-six miles,' she lives inauthentically," writes sports psychologist Carole Oglesby. She goes on to add that although few women will become Olympians, they must find this out for themselves, or they have not lived fully.

In "Letters to a Young Poet," Rilke recalled the ancient myths in which dragons symbolize fear. "Perhaps all the dragons of our lives are princesses who are only waiting to see us once beautiful and brave. Perhaps everything terrible is in its deepest being something helpless that wants help from us."

The obstacles are surmountable, the fear is merely our venture into foreign territory. The race may be difficult, but not impossible. In the end it is a friend, and nothing to fear.

24

Mental Preparation

COMPETITION is 50 percent physical, 50 percent mental—with an extra percentage of guts thrown in. Some variation of this motto is often quoted by those who test themselves in competition. It's the mind and the heart, as well as the body, that determine success in sports. The world is full of champion runners who while not blessed with the perfect physical attributes to succeed, have nonetheless triumphed—mostly by what is in their heads, not their legs. Perhaps no sport more than distance running provides greater opportunities for improvement through mental will and desire, because as every coach will tell you, sprinters are born but distance runners are made.

The ability to employ mental effort successfully requires confidence, concentration, and practice; and unlike great physical ability, with which you are born, mental preparation is a skill that must be learned. The more coaches and psychologists study athletics, the more they realize how great a factor the mind is in determining athletic success. In fact, the mind is perhaps the most underdeveloped muscle in sports. For women the "mental psych" for competition is usually even more difficult, as they have not been socialized to understand it. It's a new tool they have to learn to use.

"Traditional women's activities, like aerobics, deemphasize competition," points out sports psychologist Linda Lewis Griffith. This is substantiated in a 1975 study that although done years ago still probably holds true for today. Males selected "to win" as their priority in sports 5 percent more than females, while females selected "play well" as their priority 5 percent more than males selected "play well." "Women must realize the psychological worth of competition," adds Griffith. This will not only equip them to participate in and enjoy sports more, but help them maximize their athletic ability. From the minute you put your foot on the starting line of a race, you realize how valuable it is to learn about what you are undertaking.

"Take a chance on being great," is what coach Tracy Sundlun tells his women runners. It means making a commitment to go for it, allowing yourself to develop and utilize your ability to its fullest potential without fear of what success may mean, or the trials you may need to undergo to achieve that success.

Whether your aims are of champion proportions, or just to improve and maximize your training, you can benefit by careful mental preparation for competition, and by understanding the contribution of your state of mind to success.

"Mental preparation is like physical preparation," says Sundlun. "You recognize the weak points and work on them, and recognize the strong points and fall back on them." Some people respond positively in a race by focusing on their competition; others are motivated by prize money in the event; and some by self-improvement. And while these aspects may aid one athlete in feeling ready for competition, they may put pressure on another, or even create crippling fear and undermine success.

Some people cannot separate their personal lives from their athletic lives, and will have a hard time running well during a troubled romance, for example. Others are so determined that nothing gets in the way of them and the finish line. Mary Decker is such a competitor. Her problem is not distraction from her aim or motivating herself, but rather controlling her zealous nature and competitive drive, which is so strong and so totally focused on an aim that if these traits could be marketed, we'd be a nation of athletic amazons! Ironically, it was her ex-husband Ron Tabb who by his own admission ran a poor race in the World Championships due to his becoming emotionally upset after an awkward meeting between them at the meet, while Mary walked away with two gold medals and an eye firmly cast on the Olympics.

What kind of woman succeeds in running? Says Sundlun, "The same person who succeeds in the rest of life. Whether a scholar, a top business person, or a great athlete, there's an exact correlation. The world belongs to the B-plus people, those who stay with it."

"Running is a very logical sport," he continues. "It takes patience, common sense, and discipline." There's one more factor he stresses: self-image. You will perform only up to your level of self-esteem. How you see yourself is largely responsible for your competitive success. *I = runner* is a simple equation; it means that I identify myself as a runner. Total identification as a runner isn't mandatory, but a coach will tell you that it does make ultimate competitive success more likely. Of course, the extent to which the definition holds true depends on your involvement, but certainly for everyone who runs there is an element of truth to $I = runner$, whether it exists at the moment a woman ties her shoes to head out for a run, or whether she is Mary Decker, who is completely defined by her sport, and through it gains identity, approval, and acceptance.

For some people it's easy to get worked up over competition—too easy. For these people, perspective is the most important mental element. One can be serious, but without perspective she will almost certainly sabotage her chances for success. One's mind, like the body, has its limit. Runners call taking their ability and resources to the limit "going to the well." Mentally a person can go to the well only so often. "You can't extend the mind that often," says Sundlun. "That's the limiting factor competitively." The mind may push the body when it's tired, but when the mental edge for competition isn't there, it usually can't be forced.

To help develop the mental edge, athletes often use what are called readying techniques. Some of these techniques are more detailed in a book called *Peak Performance—Mental Game Plans for Maximizing Your Athletic Potential* by David R. Kauss. Using the following categories as a guide, you can develop your own personal readying strategy for competition, and then by practicing it, learn to understand the way your mind controls what you do.

1. *Relaxation*—It's a proven fact that the failure to relax will undermine any athletic effort. Tension and panic cause the muscles to contract, much the way they do at the end of a race when the body, like a car, runs out of gas. A tight muscle will simply not be able to perform as it should. Relaxation also helps a person to concentrate, focus on the task at hand, and best utilize the gains made in practice.

Discover what helps you to relax. Take slow, rhythmic breaths; sit alone; jog around; shake out your limbs; roll your head. Each method of relaxation has its own technique, and each runner has a personal ritual.

Some of the world's top track and field athletes can often be seen before competition placing their fingertips lightly on their forehead. This is done to calm the emotional centers—a process which does not necessarily alleviate the nervous or negative thoughts before competition, but rather renders them less harmful to performance by teaching the body to relax and gain control over fear or negativity.

2. *Positive imagery*—In order to succeed you must believe you can. This is where positive thinking comes into play, and it is developed by a technique called visualization. Create positive images of your performance; practice seeing yourself succeed in detail. Take your mind through the stages you will experience in the race.

Goal setting is an important part of visualization. It is essential that an athlete set both long- and short-range goals, which help to motivate and focus training toward a specific end. The more specific the end, the more concrete the goal, the better the inspiration. Many top athletes use signs or other visible reminders to stay constantly aware of their target.

3. *The feeling*—Unique to all of us is our own special way of feeling that means we're ready. You can achieve it by recalling a memory, image, emotion, or preparation ritual which gives you "the feeling." Some runners talk about being hungry; others have a tendency to be calm and withdrawn, while some just have an intangible "itch." Recall the good feelings of a successful workout or other experience, and try to recreate those feelings.

If "the feeling" ever had a look, it was best displayed by Eamonn Coghlan of Ireland on his way to winning the 5,000 meters in the 1983 World Championships. On the final turn, when he knew he had the victory, he clenched his fists, gritted his teeth, and looked skyward. "It's mine!" was the name of the feeling.

4. *Attention clearing and focusing (concentration)*—This is called your "mental set," which you use to focus your attention on the competition by blocking out distraction and living within the moment. The race is not the time to think of the dentist appointment you forgot to make, what is left to do at work, or what is waiting for you at home. A successful frame of mind focuses you on the present with the precision and centering of an electronic eye. Great competitors block out other events, sounds, and any other distractions so that the periphery of their field of concentration is blank or dark, as if a beam of light were focused directly in front of them on what they have to do.

5. *Planning and study*—This refers to understanding your sport and competition, planning for practice and workouts, and mental rehearsal. You can learn to understand competition by experiencing it, as well as by studying it as you would anything else: by reading about it, going to race clinics, and listening to the advice of more experienced or elite runners and coaches. Training sessions also serve as mental as well as physical rehearsals of what you will experience in a race.

According to David Kauss, becoming a good competitor and making the most of your ability are not inborn traits as many may believe. They are not even dependent on personality type, but rather involve what Kauss calls states of mind, which are specifically practiced thoughts and emotions you use to ready yourself for competition.

Mental ability, like physical ability, is something which can be developed to its maximum potential by practice. We have all heard of the power of the mind, and the race gives us a chance to test it. But never forget that we all have limits. Sometimes, as boxing champion Larry Holmes says, "Your mind makes promises your body can't keep." The art is to balance mind and body, not to overwhelm one with the other.

25

America's Running Corporations

A WOMAN RUNNER may still have problems being accepted by society—adjusting to a world which may find her avocation at best frivolous—but in the business world she has made strides as great as those she's made on the roads. In fact, in more than a few major corporations, the woman runner is respected and admired; most important, she's noticed.

Running can truly be considered an integral part of the American lifestyle when runners are supported on the job, and when companies reward their athletic efforts. By supporting the individual athlete, a company makes fitness a part of its collective identity, and becomes known as pro-health and pro-employee. So following the fitness trend works for everyone, the employees as well as the company.

Participation in corporate fitness stems from both the employees' interest and the company's concern with its own welfare. When it was revealed that the combination of sedentary life and business pressures had created a nation of physically and emotionally distressed citizens, business was prevailed upon to help solve the problem. Many companies now offer opportunities and incentives for employees to get fit, including organized workouts, daily exercise breaks, health club discounts, and even health club facilities located at the work site.

In addition, when studies revealed that a physically fit worker is more productive than his or her unfit counterpart, companies began to realize it was in everyone's interest to ensure that workers are in top shape. American business looked toward its counterparts overseas, and the evidence was clear. In Japan, for example, a country well known for its high productivity, fitness is a top company priority. In fact, elite Japanese athletes are supported by the companies they work for, and looked upon with honor and respect. The Japanese system is testimony that a fit and healthy worker is also a more productive one. A prime supporter of this theory in the United States is Jess Bell of Bonne Belle in Ohio. A runner whose company sponsors a major women's race, Bell's firm has a 2-mile track, group runs, and financial incentives for staying in shape.

Since the late seventies, corporations have been encouraged to "get running" by the emergence of corporate competitions. The world's largest corporate race is the Corporate Challenge, sponsored by Manufacturers Hanover Trust.

In 1977, only 200 people from 50 companies ran the race in Central Park. Today the number has swelled to 10,000 participants from 650 companies. In addition, the event is now conducted in three upstate New York loations and in six other major cities in the United States, and has been run in Hong Kong. Thirty-five to forty percent of the participants are women, and according to race officials that number is on the rise.

Corporate team scoring is divided into men's, women's, and coed. Three separate 3.5-mile races are held, two for men and a third for women. The event began for fun and fitness, but it now has an air of serious competition which rivals that on Wall Street. It is rumored that some companies even go so far as to hire fast runners as an ultimate recruitment tactic. However, most participants claim the race is all in fun, and that they do it mostly for the camaraderie it develops with their coworkers.

Barbara Paddock, director of special events for Manufacturers Hanover, is in charge of the Corporate Challenge. A marathoner herself, she sees tremendous value in the event for company morale and reputation. "Involvement in the Corporate Challenge puts the company in a different light than as just a corporation or business. It makes it more humanistic by putting the employees in the forefront. Sure the bottom line is production, but how a company gets there is through good morale on the part of its workers."

How women runners are treated on the job—their status, and the encouragement or rewards they receive—is a good indication of the effect a woman athlete has on the world around her, and how she in turn is affected by her surroundings.

Anna Noel is 23 years old and the captain of her Corporate Challenge team at Avon. Avon is well known in the running community for its sponsorship of major women's road races worldwide, yet Anna says surprisingly few of the two thousand Avon employees even realize the company sponsors races, nor do they know of the existence of the five-person sports department.

Avon's employee relations department has organized yoga classes and workouts for runners, which they publicize in a company newsletter. However, according to Anna, recruitment for the Corporate Challenge was done informally, by a poster in the cafeteria and word of mouth. At least one hundred Avon employees run, and many of them take advantage of the fitness classes. Most of them are women, although the company is comprised of both sexes. "It wasn't that the emphasis was on women's fitness. When the classes were offered, that's just who came," explains Anna.

For some of the Avon women, the Corporate Challenge was their first race, and even if they did the event in little more than a jog, they were ecstatic that they could go the distance. Anna, who beat some of the Avon men, claims these men view her differently now. "They're impressed I can beat them in a race. They respect me more."

Most women who run the Corporate Challenge say their companies support them, but in varying degrees. Diana Sheridan, a 33-year-old assistant branch manager at Union Mutual Life Insurance Company, ran the race at a creditable 7-minute pace, after which twenty-five of the fifty people in her office went out for a party. Her reward for running well is the recognition she gets. "Recognition is a big thing to people," she says. Although Diana has run a number of marathons, she isn't given any special consideration on the job for her running, and has no time to train for the marathon right now. However, she has no complaints about running perks. "I'm just happy the company gives us what it does."

Service-oriented or smaller companies seem to give more benefits and status to their runners than larger corporations. While most companies feature the Corporate Challenge results in the company newsletter and provide runners with company running outfits, others take it a step further with health club membership discounts and sports breaks. Rodale Press, the publisher of *Prevention* magazine, does well in the Corporate Challenge. The company allows at least two half-hour "energy breaks" a day for workouts, and a health club is located at the company site. In addition, Rodale pays workers $5 for every pound they lose.

Some executives have a real interest in creating the marriage of sport and work, and willingly admit it. Mitch Kurz, an avid 50-mile-a-week runner, is the Corporate Challenge team captain for Young & Rubicam, the largest advertising agency in the world in 1983 in terms of income.* He is

*Advertising Age, March 16, 1983.

also vice president management supervisor, and does company hiring. When he gets a resume, Mitch admits he reads down to the "additional interests" section and immediately notices if the applicant is a runner. "A jock who has a degree can't be all bad," he says only half-jokingly.

Her running was one of the things he noticed about Liz Levy, who was hired for a summer internship at the agency. Mitch reports that Liz, a top runner for many years, is beating all her clients at her new job with Levi Strauss in San Francisco. "They love it," he claims. "Her Harvard business school background is obviously a part of her success, but her running hasn't hurt. It's given her noticeability, status, and respect."

Advertising agencies are looking for people to enhance their environment with extras, and especially in a generation of physical fitness, being an athlete is important. "You have to stay on top of trends, or you're not doing your job in this business," contends Mitch.

For Young & Rubicam, the Corporate Challenge has provided camaraderie and some unique incentives. Team runners meet the president of the company, "a big thrill for most of them, who would otherwise probably be here for twenty years and never meet him," claims Mitch.

Mitch makes a significant comparison. "If a woman has run a 2:55 marathon, she's put in a lot of dedication and desire. She'll probably be a valuable member of a company, and have good characteristics for management." Finally, in support of an extracurricular activity like running he says, "In this field being smart is not enough. You have to be smart plus."

Barbara Paddock believes that women who do well in the Corporate Challenge "are more noticed. They take on a different posture—both physically and emotionally. It helps them to be more confident and assertive."

One thing is certain: their accomplishments are not going unnoticed. In a questionnaire distributed by Manufacturers Hanover to Corporate Challenge participants, the results clearly showed that senior management is very aware of employee participation in the event. And across the board, companies support runners by such gestures as paying the race entry fee and buying team outfits.

But recognition on the job isn't what all women runners want. Sarah Quinn, a 25-year-old research assistant at Morgan Guaranty Trust, has won two Corporate Challenge races. A competitor since college, she also has achieved a top-ranking 2:39 marathon time and a tenth-place finish in the 1981 New York City Marathon.

Sarah claims that not only has her running had little effect on her job, she prefers it that way. She does get moral support from the twenty-five members of her division who participated in the Corporate Challenge, and has been written up in the company newsletter, but it is important to her that she is judged on the job as a professional and not because of her running. "Running gets to be too big a deal," claims Sarah, who discovered what the sport meant to her when she started to run for money. "I don't want it to be my profession. I don't like doing it for anything or anyone else but myself."

Barbara Paddock cautions that the corporate/athlete relationship has to be kept in perspective. She says that these days serious men and women athletes sometimes come into corporations expecting unlimited time off to train. She also questions how a serious runner, who must devote so much time to training, can perform well in a full-time business position.

Despite the few possible problems of corporate running for both the company and the employee, the day of the Corporate Challenge race is the best testimony to the value of a close relationship between sport and work.

By race time, Central Park is filled with shouting, enthusiastic team members, proudly dressed in company outfits and taking team photos. When the horn sounds signaling the start of the race, supporters take their places along the course and at the finish line to cheer for their teammates. The sound of company names rings through the park like a roll call of the Fortune 500.

After the event, teammates scatter to bars, restaurants, or apartments around the city to celebrate and to brag or lament over their race. Men and women together, from company president on down—on this day they are the best they could ever wish to be; they are equal.

26

Major Women's Races*

AVON INTERNATIONAL RUNNING CIRCUIT

Avon conducts the most comprehensive women's running program, featuring a series of clinics and women-only races in nineteen countries, including the United States, Puerto Rico, Canada, Germany, England, France, Australia, Chile, Brazil, the Netherlands, the Philippines, Japan, Belgium, New Zealand, Mexico, Malaysia, Thailand, Argentina, and Spain. The circuit, composed of races ranging from 5 kilometers (3.1 miles) to the marathon, culminates every year in the Avon International Marathon Championship. The event held on June 5, 1983, was run along 90 percent of the route of the 1984 women's Olympic marathon, and served as a qualifier for the American women's marathon team to the World Championships in Helsinki. The Avon Marathon in Paris, France, on September 23, 1984, offers one of the largest purses of developmental training money, $65,000.

Avon races, including the marathon championship, are open to all women. There are no qualifying standards or limits, except an age minimum of 14 in the marathon in keeping with the policy of the sport's governing body. The top fifteen finishers in any Avon race receive points which entitle them to earn an expense-paid trip to the marathon championship.

The Avon circuit is the brainchild of Kathrine Switzer, known for her Boston Marathon run of 1967, in which a race official tried to throw her off

*For information on any of these races check the Resource List for the addresses of the organizers.

the course. Switzer now oversees a program in which 100,000 women compete in races around the world.

In addition to events with 1,000 to 2,000 runners in such cities as Atlanta, New York, Kansas City, Chicago, and Los Angeles, Avon has staged races which include women from over thirty-one nations. Some of these races have drawn impressive numbers and are held in such spots as Brasília (5,000 women), Tokyo (over 1,000), Santiago (4,832), and Bangkok (1,659).

Ironically, before the staging of these events, Avon organizers were often told that women in these countries just don't run. But the story of the Avon 10-kilometer race in São Paulo, Brazil, on August 8, 1983, proves all the skeptics wrong, and illustrates the desire and talent of women runners everywhere.

Of the 6,547 women who entered the race, making it one of the largest women's race ever, several remarkable times were recorded, and under remarkable circumstances. Following the winner, American Kathy Molitor-Barton in 35:48, were two Brazilian sisters, ages 13 and 11, who came home in 36:22 and 36:23—running barefoot! To top it off, their 9-year-old sister came in ninth, in 38:05. These times would rank high in any women's race, and in the United States these girls would have college recruiters offering them full scholarships before they even reached high school.

The Avon series has shown that women everywhere are eager and able to run and, together with other women's races, has helped gain approval for women's international and Olympic running events.

BONNE BELL

The Bonne Bell 10-kilometer race, the largest women's race series in the United States, is conducted in eighteen major cities around the country, culminating in the championship held every October on Columbus Day in Boston.

The series began in 1977 with five cities, and has grown every year since, to a record number of 33,000 participants in 1983. The Boston championship included 2,300 its first year in 1977 and almost 8,000 in 1983. Every year the winners of the other Bonne Bell races are brought to the final, all expenses paid. The quality of the event is evident in the records that have been set in the championship. Every year to date the Boston race has produced an American 10-kilometer road record (except 1982, when New Zealand's Anne Audain won with a course record). Joan Benoit was the 1983 winner, with an American record time of 31:36. Plans for the race series in 1984 and beyond include additional race clinics, and in cooperation with cosponsors Brooks and Chevrolet, a women's triathlon and a Bonne Bell Running Camp.

The race is an outgrowth of the personal philosophy of Jess Bell, president of Bonne Bell Cosmetics and a runner and avid fitness enthusiast who built one of the original and most extensive employee fitness programs in the country in his company's Ohio headquarters. He began the women's series when he noticed that a mere 5 percent of the field were women in the races when he began running. Although Bonne Bell has long been involved in sports sponsorship, with such ventures as the U.S. Ski Team and tennis, judging by the correspondence of those who participate, women's running is by far its most successful and rewarding sponsorship.

According to Bonne Bell race coordinator Ben Barron, the philosophy behind the event is that although top competition and records are important, it's the numbers of women that provide the most satisfaction to the sponsors. He says the race is especially important for the substantial number of those who feel more comfortable in an all-women's event.

"Be fit. Look good," is the motto of Bonne Bell's fitness program, and the company claims, "We not only believe it, we live it!" According to Ben Barron, Bonne Bell has earned the right to its special status as a women's race series as the company is not just a sponsor, but wholeheartedly believes in the principles of fitness and tries to live them with its corporate programs.

EVENING PRESS/BROOKS WOMEN'S MINI MARATHON

Imagine a race in the United States with 547,000 women. That is the equivalent ratio of the number of Irish women who ran in the Mini Marathon. Eight thousand women, the largest field ever assembled, ran 10 kilometers through the streets of Dublin on June 12, 1983. This is remarkable not only for a first-time event, but because the population of Ireland is a mere 3.5 million. That means that approximately 1 out of every 219 Irish women ran the race!

"It was simply fantastic!" intoned the *Evening Press*, one of Ireland's largest newspapers and a sponsor of the event. A front-page headline the day after the race declared, "A giant leap forward by 8,000 women. . . ."

Katy Schilly of the United States hit the tape for first in 34:04, followed by 2:29-marathoner Carey May, the Irish national record holder, who flew home from the United States at the last minute to take part in the event. The next six places went to top Irish runners.

The significance of the race cannot be overstated. Not only did it showcase Ireland's best women runners, but completing the 6.2 miles were grandmothers, handicapped women, a long list of journalists, housewives, and even Ireland's women's affairs minister, who wore her finisher's medal before her colleagues the following week to prove she had gone the distance.

The impact of women's running is truly realized when on the front page of a major daily newspaper one can read: "One little girl hugged her middle-aged Mum who was proudly wearing the medallion given to everyone who finished, while her father took pictures."

THE L'EGGS MINI MARATHON

"Who Says Women Can't Run The World?" is the slogan of the L'eggs Mini Marathon, a 10-kilometer (6.2-mile) event that bills itself "the original and most prestigious road race for women only." In 1983, 5,899 women followed in the fleet footsteps of winner Anne Audain of New Zealand, who broke the tape in 32:23, handing Grete Waitz her first defeat in five Central Park Minis.

The event began in 1972—the first women-only road race in the world—as a 6-miler with 78 entries called the Crazy Legs Mini Marathon. In 1977, the year after the New York City Marathon went from Central Park out into the streets of New York and helped raise running consciousness, the entries in the Mini went from 492 to 2,277. In 1978, the numbers shot up to 4,346, and L'eggs products became the sponsor. Along came Grete Waitz in 1979, and by 1982 she had collected a string of four victories and two 10-kilometer world road records. Her phenomenal record of 30:59:8 has yet to be approached by any woman, and this time would win many men's races.

In the early years of the Mini most of the runners were from the New York area and all were in their late teens or early 20s—high school or club athletes. With the widespread popularity of road running, and a concentrated effort by race organizers to develop women's running with clinics and developmental runs, women everywhere and from all backgrounds began to enter the race. By 1983, runners in the Mini came from thirty-four states and eight countries. They ranged in age from 6 to 72, and they represented close to 100 different professions—from 583 teachers to 2 company presidents to 1 mechanic. These women were learning that they too could "go the distance."

The race is run as a series, with the final event held in New York in May or June. Other races in the series, called the L'eggs–YWCA 10-kilometer, are held in San Diego in February, Chicago in April, and Dallas in September. These events draw anywhere from 900 to 2,000 women, and the winners are brought to the New York event all expenses paid. In 1984 the aim is to encourage women who have never run a race. In addition to the usual prerace clinic, an educational clinic and fun run will be held several months prior to the final event.

Thousands of balloons head for the sky as the starting horn sounds, and women compete for awards, against the clock, or just to finish. Every finisher gets a medal and there are special awards for the top women in all age groups, teams, mother/daughter duos, and sisters. In 1983, a record seven sisters in the Kelly family ran the race, while their mother organized a family picnic. The Mini is definitely women's day.

FIRST WOMEN'S OLYMPIC MARATHON TRIALS

On May 12, 1984, every American woman who had run a certified marathon during the previous year (from April 1, 1983, to April 16, 1984) in 2:51:16 or better was entitled to a shot at the women's Olympic marathon team at the first women's Olympic marathon trials. The qualifying time was based on the hundredth-fastest time by an American woman in 1982, the same way it is determined for men. Appropriately, they ran in Olympia, Washington, on a flat, loop course, where the top three finishers made the Olympic team. An hour of the event was broadcast live, coast to coast, by ABC Sports, the network of the Olympics.

The top 200 qualifiers, the majority of women who met the standard, were provided with expense-paid trips to the trials and room and board for up to six days. In an effort to duplicate the Olympic Games, a special Olympic Village was created in a nearby college and a week of Olympic-style festivities preceded the race.

According to race director Brent James, the aim was to provide every one of the trials participants with an Olympic experience. "The objective was to give a taste of what the Olympics is like and to give that opportunity for even the two-hundredth woman who would ordinarily never have that experience." More than just a race, he envisioned it as an event. "The real purpose of the race was to create a showcase for the significant achievements women have made in sports."

FIRST WOMEN'S OLYMPIC MARATHON

It took the excellence of a new generation of women runners and the lobbying of many concerned organizations to convince the International Olympic Committee (IOC) and the IAAF that there should be a women's Olympic marathon. On August 5, 1984, at 8 a.m., the long-awaited event happens for the first time.

From 150 to 225 of the best women marathoners will probably compete in the race, representing close to twenty-five nations. The women's race will probably have about fifty fewer competitors than the men's marathon because certain countries strong in distance running are still without women participants, notably the African nations.

According to Olympic rules, every country is allowed at least one contestant for each track and field event, and a maximum of three for those who meet qualifying standards. For the marathon, however, there is no Olympic qualifying standard, as each race course varies. Therefore, each country will send from one to three of its best marathoners, regardless of their times. In fact, there are no official world records for the marathon. As with all road races, the times are technically called world bests.

The route of the Olympic marathon begins at Santa Monica Community College, 16 miles from the finish in Olympic Stadium. According to the chief referee of the Olympic marathon Allan Steinfeld, the aim is to avoid the Los Angeles pollution "by being outside the city and getting as much good air as possible." Steinfeld reports that the point-to-point course, run on several main thoroughfares, features a long straightaway for the last six or seven miles. During the toughest portion of the race the runners can always see a never-ending stretch before them. "It can be demoralizing," admits Steinfeld. By this point, however, the top women probably won't notice, as they will be locked in a tactical battle for an Olympic medal.

Everything will be carefully prepared for the women in this historic event. In keeping with the rules, separate refreshment and sponge stations will be set up at least every 5 kilometers (3.1 miles). To the detail the women will have the best. "This country's top officials will work the race.

Thirteen of them have already measured the course. It's the most accurate measurement ever done," boasts Steinfeld.

The worldwide television coverage of the race is significant, as most people will be exposed to an event which has gotten relatively little coverage. According to Bob Iger of ABC Sports, because the event is tied to a social phenomenon, it will receive special treatment on the air. "This isn't just any event. There's a much greater story to tell about the significance of women's emergence in a sport. We have an obligation to tell that story."

27

Safety Tips
for Women Runners

YOU'RE RUNNING through a quiet, tree-lined area. Your mind is on nothing at all, and you feel like you're flying. We all know the sensation—it's one of the reasons we run. But suddenly, from some corner or path you didn't see, a stranger comes running toward you. Your mind is called back to attention; your eye is riveted on the approaching figure. Your heart begins to beat in your ears like a brass band. The stranger passes. It's over. You're safe. This time. But you realize once again: you're not free.

No, women aren't free, and none of us can afford to be part of the bucolic scene outlined above. Henley Roughton, author of a women's running column, claims it's easy to succumb to a false sense of security. However, attacks are all too common. The Washington RunHers conducted a survey of 128 women concerning attacks. Two out of every five respondents had been threatened by a man or men while running.

We should not run alone, in deserted areas, or near tree-lined paths. We should not let our minds wander aimlessly. This is a fact of life, both urban and rural. There are some basic safety rules and conditions we must learn to live by, no matter where we run and who we are, but especially if we are women.

Detective Lucille Burrascano of the New York City Police Department's crime prevention section knows the score. A detective for seventeen years, she has learned the rules of the game the hard way: practical experience on the street. The following advice is part of a lecture she gave at the New York Road Runners Club. Her tips are highlighted in a pamphlet entitled

"Safety Tips for Runners," compiled by the Road Runners and the police department.* The advice is important for anyone in any location—not just for runners.

Contrary to what we often think about big cities, New York, with the largest concentration of runners anywhere, happens to be one of the safest places in which to run. Runners and running organizations have lobbied long and hard to provide additional police protection and better lighting, and work closely with the police department to maintain the best safety conditions possible. If you have a problem in your area, or a potential one, don't hesitate to contact a local running club or your police department to get help.

Tips   Reduce the opportunity of your being the target. Run with one or several companions. There is safety in numbers. Although this is the cardinal rule of running safety, of the 939 women who answered the question in the survey for this book, only a meager 26 never run alone (340 said they always run alone, and 547 said they sometimes do). Yet a reported 98 percent of the attacks against women happen when they are alone. And they can occur at any time of the day, and by anyone.

> • Run relaxed and confident yet aware of your surroundings. Entering the "other world" associated with running is absolutely against the principles of crime prevention. You have got to be in the here and now, paying attention to your surroundings, in order to take care of yourself.

> • Create a "safety area" around yourself within which no one should enter. This personal space should be defended at all times from intrusion. Your personal space, says Burrascano, is for lovers or spouses, not strangers. If someone is too close, move away.

> • Know the area in which you run. Have several emergency escape routes planned at intervals along your running route. Be familiar with nearby inhabited areas or where help may be obtained. Know where there are police call boxes or telephones.

> • Avoid running adjacent to dense foliage or places from which you can be set upon without warning. Run in well-lighted areas if possible.

*A copy of this pamphlet may be obtained by sending a self-addressed stamped envelope to the New York Road Runners Club, P.O. Box 1388, GPO, 10116. Write "Safety Tips" on the lower left-hand corner of your envelope.

• Anger is a good control weapon. When you are approached, spontaneous anger can intimidate, buy time, or give a potential attacker second thoughts. A positive posture and aggressive attitude are far more of a deterrent than passive and timid body language and behavior. Body language works. Don't cower or look frightened. You're a serious athlete, with a right to be out running, and you must communicate that in your stride.

Anger is a subject that deserves elaboration. You may have to practice learning automatic, angry responses, and if you are confronted by a rapist, anger may be your best weapon. "A rapist wants a woman who is passive," reports Detective Burrascano. "Rape is a crime of power, not sexual gratification. A rapist wants to overpower, possess, and humiliate you because he is helpless and powerless in his own life. An aggressive woman intimidates a rapist."

Get angry, and if you are worried about offending someone, it's better to growl and apologize later. "Give it your all," says Burrascano, "even profanity. God will forgive you if you curse." If you are confronted by an unarmed attacker, quickly and without warning flee. If this is not possible, display anger by yelling such responses as "GET AWAY FROM ME," while at the same time quickly retreating via one of your emergency escape routes. "There is nothing wrong with being mad," adds Burrascano. "Crime is rude. We women have got to learn to be angry."

Flashers and masturbators are another issue. Don't do anything when you encounter them. They are trying to get a reaction from you, so just ignore them. Do, however, report the incident to the police.

"In most rape avoidance cases, the woman fought like crazy when the attack first started," according to Burrascano. Keep in mind that you can successfully fight off the rape, but you still might get hurt. If you are forced to fight, remember the following:

• As a last resort render quick, disabling blows and retreat. Practice attacks to the groin, eyes, and throat, which are meant to disable, and are usually more effective than cursory scratching, punching, and kicking, which often escalate the attacker's response.

"Crime is very terrifying, but right here and now you must decide what you're going to do, and be prepared to react immediately," says Detective Burrascano. You do have two things in your favor: you are in good shape, and you are dressed to fight. If you do decide to fight, do it effectively. Hitting the bone up the nose is disabling, as is going for the eyes. If you hit to the groin, do it straight up between the legs, not from the front. The point of the blow is to render the attacker helpless, and a blow to the testicles is much more painful than one to the penis. Remember, you cannot wait until five minutes into the attack, you must fight from the minute you are grabbed. "Most women see rape as a crime of mutilation or murder but the vast majority of rapes are simply for the purpose of humiliating the victim," according to Detective Burrascano. If you have considered carrying a weapon, understand that you must be prepared to use it, and know how. If it is not in your hand ready to be used, it's too late to go for it after you're already confronted. Don't forget that if the attacker finds the weapon first, there may be trouble. So Burrascano recommends you consider the usefulness or practicality before considering running with a weapon.

You should be aware that rapists are getting more refined. They may be dressed in three-piece suits, or approach you and in a soft voice ask for the time or directions—trying to get you to move closer to strike up a conversation. The rule you learned as a child still applies: don't talk to strangers.

This may not be a pleasant subject, but it is important, and education and knowledge will help you protect yourself. I have found that there are some other effective strategies if you are caught in a potentially dangerous situation, whether running or not. If you suspect you're not safe in someone's company, begin to act strangely: sing to yourself, cry, dig in a nearby garbage can, pretend to be sick, or if necessary and you are able, force yourself to throw up. This type of behavior that can turn someone off may buy you time. It's no guarantee, but I have escaped dangerous situations this way, and know others who have as well.

If you must run alone, go where there are people, or hook up with a group. If I am alone and approaching the deserted side of Central Park, for example, I stop and wait for another runner, or turn around and head the other way. "We don't want to admit we're afraid," says Detective Burrascano. "Admit it. No one wants to be a crime victim. 'I'm going there alone; I'm not going to worry,' is just dumb thinking."

• Reduce the opportunity of your property being the target. Dress to run. Don't carry or wear attractive theft items such as jewelry, radios, earphones, or expensive clothing.

Don't think you're safe by assuming your $25 running watch or old earrings are junk—a robber doesn't know their value. Try to wear as little as possible, and leave the walkman-type radios at home. "The less you have, the less of a target you become," says Detective Burrascano.

Robbery requires a different tactic than rape. If a robber with a gun asks for your money, give it to him. Detective Burrascano believes robberies that result in injury to the victim occur because the robber has been provoked by verbal abuse. "Don't preach to robbers; they know they're bad," she says. And no matter how many crimes the robber commits, he is still nervous. Do not fight with an armed attacker when property is the intended target; your life is worth more than property.

• If you are confronted or attacked, observe as much as you can about the criminal(s). Notice any details that will aid you in describing them and their mannerisms. When trying to determine age, height, weight, and appearance, make comparisons between them and yourself or people you know.

Call the police as soon as possible. (Know the emergency number in your area.) The sooner the crime is reported, the greater the chance that the criminal(s) will be in the vicinity and can be apprehended.

Prevention is the key, and the rules seem easy to follow, yet women run alone and in dangerous areas in everything from pearls to $80 walkmans. Even warning them often doesn't help; they don't seem to want their freedom hampered. "I will not tell you to stop living your life," concludes Detective Burrascano, "but live it carefully."

28

Tips for the Road

THE FOLLOWING are some other general safety tips for all runners to keep in mind. Most of these tips are recommendations by the Road Runners Club of America and Dannon Yogurt.

- Whenever possible, run on roads with wide shoulders, thereby avoiding running in the street.
- Make the first move when a car is coming toward you. You should not expect the car to move for you. Run defensively.
- Always wear reflective or light-colored garments at night so drivers can see you easily. Some running shoes and most nylon running suits feature reflective strips. If your gear does not, you can buy reflective tape to adhere to shoes and clothes, or a specially made reflective vest for running in the dark.
- Try to run on smooth surfaces. This will help prevent foot injuries like twisted or sprained ankles.
- Run single file when there is a lot of traffic.
- Be careful on blind curves, and keep an eye on cars stopped at intersections which you are crossing.
- Do not "challenge" cars. A toot of the horn should be acknowledged with a wave of the hand and not with derision.
- When snow accumulation leaves no clear path alongside the road, and there is only a narrow, cleared lane for cars, you should not run in that cleared part of the road. Find an alternate place to run, even if it's around one clear block, or you might run up sets of stairs in your home or apartment building.

- If a driver purposely tries to hit you, he or she has broken the law. Memorize the license number, make, and model of the car. Try to obtain a brief description of the driver. Swear out a warrant for the highest possible offense with the local police.
- Carry ID when you run. If there is an accident or a health problem, some kind of identification could save your life. If you prefer not to run with your name and address because you are carrying your keys, write your phone number and the number(s) of a relative or close friend.

HOT-WEATHER RUNNING TIPS*

Summer heat and humidity can cause hyperthermia—body temperatures of 105 degrees and over which stop the body's temperature control system. Hyperthermia (muscle cramps, heat exhaustion, heatstroke) can be deadly. The symptoms are dizziness, dry skin—no sweating, redness, nausea or cramps, goose bumps or a cold feeling, and incoherent speech and thoughts. When any of these symptoms occur, stop running immediately. Hyperthermia can affect any runner, no matter what shape he or she is in, and can happen during temperatures of 60 degrees as well as 90 degrees, depending on the humidity.

- *Wear cool clothing.* Light-colored (to reflect sunlight), loose, sleeve-less shirts of 100 percent cotton or nylon and cotton mesh are best. Shorts of nylon or other lightweight material that does not chafe are recommended, as are cotton socks, and headbands if perspiration interferes with vision.

- *Drink plenty of fluids.* On very hot or humid days, the body's natural cooling process of sweating and evaporation can stop. Drink before you get thirsty, preferably water (before, during, and after a run), anywhere from 1–3 quarts a day.

- *Don't run in the midday sun.* Early morning or late evening are preferable times, and morning is even better to avoid summer pollution. If you do run in bright sunshine, a hat with a visor will help shield you from the sun. Wetting the hat is a way to keep cooler. In the

---

*For copies of flyers on hot- or cold-weather running tips, send a self-addressed stamped envelope to the New York Road Runners Club. Write the the name of the flyer(s) you want on the lower left-hand corner of the envelope.

event of overheating, cold water or ice placed on the carotid arteries (pulse in front of the neck) is the fastest way to bring down body temperature.

• *Replenish your body's supply of minerals.* Magnesium and potassium, in particular, are lost through sweating. Fresh fruits and vegetables, especially bananas, watermelon, cantaloupe, carrots, and tomatoes, contain essential elements, or you may try one of the commercially produced electrolyte replacement drinks made for athletes.

• *Use common sense.* If it's hot, don't run a race "all out," and if you can avoid it, skip racing. Lower your expectations for time and distance in the heat. Remember, as in all temperature extremes, your body is working harder in the heat.

COLD-WEATHER RUNNING TIPS *

Cold weather is no reason to halt your running routine, or even put off beginning to run, but certain precautions should be taken.

As in other climatic extremes, it takes the body approximately two weeks to adjust to cold-weather running. You may want to be a bit conservative at first if you are not used to the cold.

Clothing Clothing should be warm but breathable. You can gauge how to dress by finding out the windchill factor as well as the temperature. Many layers of clothing are best, as they can be taken off if you get warm (you can tie them around your waist). Up to 40 percent of the body's overall heat is lost through the head. Wear a close-fitting woolen ski-type hat. Mittens are preferable to gloves as the fingers can warm each other if held together. Woolen socks are often worn on the hands for warmth and breathability. Clothing made of 100 percent wool is good, as it breathes and wicks moisture to the surface for evaporation; however, polypropylene is best for wearing closest to the skin and polyester is the second-best. A turtleneck shirt or sweater keeps the neck warm as well. The legs need less protection as they are generating the most heat. Nylon running pants over wool or tights are good for keeping the wind out. Gortex, another material designed for winter running, is rain and cold-proof and allows perspiration to escape.

* See footnote, p. 158.

Hypothermia   Hypothermia is a drop in body temperature. It is important to get dry and warm as soon as possible if hypothermia occurs. If you experience any feeling out of the ordinary (excessive chill or numbness), don't run through it; find shelter and warmth as soon as possible. Beware of the combination of wet clothes and cold temperatures. Run against the wind on the way out, and with the wind on the way back, so as not to be chilled by perspiration that has formed during running. On very cold days, let someone know where you are running and when you expect to return.

Frostbite   Frostbite usually occurs to ears, face, fingers, and toes. The skin becomes swollen, white, or numb. Precautions against frostbite include covering extremities like ears and fingers with hats and mittens, and perhaps the use of Frostgard. Vaseline aids against a cold face or other exposed skin.

Although people sometimes fear that running in cold weather can damage their lungs, this is not possible. The lungs warm air sufficiently as it enters. If the cold air is uncomfortable to breathe, though, a face mask or ski hat that covers the nose and surrounds the mouth may help.

If it is getting out that is the hardest for you, warm up indoors first to get the blood flowing. If the streets are icy, the footing is dangerous, or you just feel it is too cold, try alternative forms of exercise. Warm up and then work out by repeatedly climbing or running up your apartment building stairs, or swim or ride a stationary bike.

Running on snow is usually no problem if you take it slow and easy. However, ice or any slippery surface should obviously be avoided. If you are worried that your training suffers from slogging in slush, remember that a slower pace in more difficult conditions is an equally tough workout as a faster pace in good conditions.

29

Running Gear

I T WASN'T many years ago that women athletes bought boys' sports clothes, did the best they could with men's shoes, and suffered the chafing and drooping straps of ill-fitting bras for their activity. Today, the shoe is literally on the other foot. According to a woman's running gear manufacturer, 60 percent of the 75 million people in the fitness market are women.

SHOES

Nothing is more important to a runner than shoes, and the latest scientific advances in shoe construction allow the modern athlete to put the body through any number of miles. According to Diane Magnani, owner of the Super Runners Shop on Manhattan's Upper West Side, almost every top model of men's running shoe is now available in women's sizes, or made in a woman's version. Diane gives the following advice for the smart woman consumer when buying running shoes.

You should consider the following questions before choosing a shoe: 1. How much running do you do? 2. What shoe are you running in now, and are you happy with it? 3. On what surfaces do you run? 4. Do you have any particular problems (e.g., pronation—the feet buckle inward)? If you are a beginner, buy shoes according to what feels good on your feet, and the price. You need not buy the top-of-the-line shoe; buy a moderately priced shoe to begin with.

You can buy a men's or women's shoe; again, choose whatever feels the best. The only difference besides color is that the women's shoe is narrower than the men's. Men's sizes are a size and a half smaller than women's. Assess fit by allowing a thumb's width for toe room, and if your feet are slightly different in length, choose the size that fits the larger foot. "Women often don't want to take a bigger size shoe," says Diane, "but a running shoe should be a half to one size larger than a street shoe." Don't cheat yourself with a smaller shoe; your toes will pay the price!

The qualities of a good running shoe are as follows: 1. good (stiff) heel counter for lateral stability, 2. good arch support, 3. cushioning, and 4. flexibility. When you try the shoe on, if possible walk on a hard surface, not on a rug. Some running shoe stores let you take the shoes out for a test run on the asphalt. Shoes will all give slightly in width, but they should be snug and comfortable from the moment you try them on. With a running shoe more than any other kind, you'll probably know right away if it's for you because it feels perfect. There is really no "breaking in" a shoe to make it feel right. And when you find a good model, stay with it. "The most important thing when purchasing a running shoe is to stay with the shoe that works for you," emphasizes Diane. "You'd think that goes without saying, but people always want to try something new."

For runners who do more than 40 miles a week, a better shoe should be purchased. The more expensive the shoe, the higher the technology. Shoes are now made with heel wraps for stability, pronation inhibitors, and several different materials in the mid-sole. According to Diane, shoe companies are now aware of women's needs, and they also realize that a woman is willing to pay the price for a good shoe, so all the latest features are available for women's shoes as well as men's.

Some other guidelines include:

- Never run in any other shoe but a running shoe. The necessary features for the activity are exclusive to a running shoe.
- Washing the shoes is not recommended, but if you feel you must, wash them by hand with warm water and mild soap.
- Never dry shoes in the sun or near a heater.
- Most runners examine the soles of the shoes to check for wear, but you can also tell if your running shoe is ready for retirement if the midsole gets compressed. If you are not sure, simply try on a new pair of shoes with the old; the old ones will feel flat. Shoes last from five hundred miles of running to a maximum of a thousand miles. Of course, the lighter racing shoes have a shorter running life.

CLOTHING

Running shorts and singlets are nylon or polyester blends. Nylon is light and dries quickly, and the addition of mesh on singlets provides good ventilation. Some singlets now feature a complete mesh back, with a nylon chest panel in front in special styles for women.

If it's cold, layered clothing is best rather than a one-piece bulky sweat suit. Tights with shorts can be worn, or cotton/polyester sweat suit pants, a nylon rain suit, or a more expensive investment—Gortex. Shirts and tights are also made of polypropylene, a light material that stays dry by allowing perspiration to evaporate.

Running bras This is probably the single most essential clothing item for a woman runner. Most sport bras are made with a cotton/polyester blend that is nonchafing and absorbent. They feature wide shoulder straps that cross in the back or form a V to stay on securely. Seams are outside, and the bra should have covered hooks or clasps, or be made without them. A wide band along the bottom keeps the bra from riding up. These bras are designed to hold the breasts close to the body to keep movement to a minimum.

Get a well-made bra that distributes the weight of the breasts evenly over the rib cage and spreads the weight over the back, rather than using the shoulders as support. This is the advice of Dr. Christine Haycock of New Jersey, who filmed women running with both sport and regular bras, as well as braless, and determined that there was greater comfort and better performance among women wearing the sport bra.

When selecting a sport or running bra, try on as many as possible. Jump up and down, swing your arms in a running motion, and then raise them and take deep breaths, expanding your rib cage. The bra should not interfere with movement or breathing. Although it should be firm, it should not be too tight.

Part IV
Predictions

30

The Future of
Women's Running

I T'S TEMPTING to imagine the future of such a fast-changing social movement as women's running, and predictions abound. The social ramifications of millions of women running are enormous. Consider the effect of the sport on an individual level and multiply it by the increasing numbers of participants. If you begin running today, what will your physical and emotional evolution be in ten years? What effect in turn will it have on your job, family, friends, or children?

Setting the trend in women's running will be the elite athlete, who will no doubt change in the future due to greater specialization of the sport and higher standards of achievement. Hers will be both a social and a technical evolution, which will in turn affect every woman.

"I think women will have to go through some of the growing stages men have gone through, like discovering the marathon is not just an endurance race but a race of speed or tactics," says Nina Kuscsik. She also believes a greater lifestyle difference will exist between the elite runner and other women. Physiological changes may result both from advanced training and from efforts to find the winning edge however possible. "Steroids may add to that lifestyle difference," cautions Kuscsik. "I think there's going to have to be some choices made that may not be in the interest of these women in the long run."

Women like Nina Kuscsik and Grete Waitz predict we will see a sub-2:20 marathon by a woman. With young talent abounding, and with the inevitable emergence of the Eastern European women in the longer distances now that they are Olympic events, today's top women runners hesitate to give any predictions on who will be out front in the future, and how fast she will run to get there. It could be a young hotshot, or a relative unknown like Grete Waitz when she set a world record. Just as today's elite woman runner is different from the one who dominated the sport ten years ago when housewives like Miki Gorman and Nina Kuscsik inadvertently discovered their interest and talent, she will surely be different in the next decade. Who knows what kind of new superathlete will emerge!

Women's running is usually analyzed by past progress, and there is no doubt about it—the records and achievements are great, especially given the short time women have been active in the sport. Scores of publications by every type of expert discuss the great strides women have made in running, and they are impressive. Charting distances from 800 meters to the marathon shows that tremendous improvement has come in waves— occurring each time women's running has gained further social acceptance and therefore further opportunities. This is particularly evident in the distances that have been added to the Olympics—the ultimate sign of acceptance. Since the 1,500 meters was added to the Games in 1972, for example, the women's world record went from 4:01:4 to the present record of 3:52:47 set in 1980, as compared to the men's record in that same eight-year span, which edged from only 3:33:1 to 3:30:77. Unlimited progress can therefore be expected for the women's marathon, for which the record time is already rapidly dropping and which is now an Olympic event. This progress will in turn generate improvement in other events.

Comparisons are made showing dramatic gains for women versus men at all distances. In fact, the average life span of a world record for men is 5.3 years, while for women it is 2.2 years. The performance gap is only 10 percent and closing, and some experts predict equal performances at all distances by men and women in 20 to 30 years.

Differences between men and women are slight in physiological requirements for distance running, which is based more on endurance rather than sheer muscle mass. Men have certain physical advantages, for example, higher overall values for maximum heart rate and VO_2 max, but their significance diminishes when a woman's smaller relative body size is taken into account.

However, it is unlikely that even a physical comparison between the sexes means much, as factors such as maximum oxygen uptake, body fat levels, and even strength have been shown to change with more intense training techniques and earlier and more frequent participation of women in sports. It is only very recently that women athletes have been studied at all, let alone objectively—without social or medical preconceptions. Findings show that males and females equally trained for endurance events have similar aerobic capacity and muscle fiber composition. At the elite level, physiological differences are reduced even further. Both men and women world class runners often have under 10 percent body fat and relatively little difference in VO_2 max—both key traits for endurance athletes.

Faster records and increased participation have generated a lot of excitement. People call these new numbers a vision for the future of women's running. Growth in women's sports is characterized as epidemic, and there is always talk about a women's running revolution. In fact, we have been led to assume that parity is if not already reached, then imminent. But has a women's running "revolution" really taken place? Aren't these expressions of grandeur and size at best deceiving, and at worst a sign that we are being lulled into accepting the status quo? Brooks Johnson thinks so, and he offers a different interpretation using the same system of analysis that other experts employ: numbers. "Progress is mathematical," he says. "When you start at zero, one becomes an infinite amount."

Starting from nothing, a little does look like a lot. But rather than content ourselves with what is, projecting the relatively small gains beyond zero which have been made, it would be much more useful to consider what must take place in order to initiate the kind of change which is truly meaningful, and which will provide true equality.

To say that women have come a long way, without realizing that the gains are relative, and to be content with this progress, is to stop short of gaining true equality by misunderstanding what equality means. Focusing on the predictions of whether women can run as fast as men is not only irrelevant, but dangerous, for it implies that women must do so in order to deserve equal opportunity.

The issue is not biological—whether women are equipped to run faster or longer than men—but moral and legal. Brooks Johnson quotes the Declaration of Independence, the most basic social law: "We hold these truths to be self-evident: that all men are created equal . . ." Equal opportunity is our birthright in sports as it is in all of life. It need not be earned by outrunning men, and should not be determined by biological standards. Until true equality is achieved, even slicing full minutes off records is an arbitrary measure. It is no guarantee that women runners will be granted equal opportunity or equal respect.

Using physiology as a measuring stick for progress is equally fallacious. After all, if we had let medical experts be our guide not so many years ago, the only exercise we'd be doing would be exercising caution to keep our inner organs from getting scrambled and our skin from sagging. Even supposedly fixed measurements like muscle and bone strength are constantly being reevaluated based on new research. And biological standards not only are the wrong guidelines for equal opportunity, but also set limits that, significantly, have never been applied to men. It is not up to others to tell us what we can or should do based on supposed physical limitations. Control of our own bodies is also part of our constitutional birthright.

The future will be determined by sociological and psychological factors, not by whether a woman beats a man to the tape because she has the lung power and the muscle mass to do so. Whether she does anyway may just depend less on the physiological differences between the sexes and more on the conditioned social differences. Besides, when true equality is achieved, it will be realized that meaningful competition is between *peers*—runner against runner—not between men and women.

Why do women in certain countries excel in sports, for example? Surely it is not because one culture is inherently more physically able than another. It is psychosocial influences that determine this development. East Germany and Russia produce more women's sports champions because women in these countries are encouraged to participate in sports and are held in high regard for their achievements. In countries such as France and Spain there is a conspicuous absence of female champions because social prejudice has created a psychological barrier to athletic achievement.

If women are to gain equality in sports, we must do it in the same way we achieve it in all other fields. "Men still have the power," says Brooks Johnson, "and nobody willingly gives up an advantageous position. Continual force has to be applied—and an increase, not a lessening of this force." So far, Johnson doesn't see that necessary energy level, and fears that women may be lulled into believing they have achieved equality by those in power.

But there's hope. "Women do have the wherewithal to create change," adds Johnson. Despite the approval of the women's Olympic marathon, for example, many people realize that without the 5,000 and 10,000 meters, women do not have equality, and these people are angry enough, smart enough, and strong enough to fight for it.

If we believe in our own limitations, we will be limited. We must always look toward the horizon, not down at the ground in front of us. We must see our ability in sports, as in life, as unlimited, or we will never approach our ultimate capabilities. As Dr. Dorothy Harris says in comparing male and female athletic capabilities, "The blueprint is the same." This is all we need: the basic equipment, and our rights as guaranteed by the Constitution.

There were 10,000 women who ran a marathon in 1980—the last year the number was counted, as it began to grow so large. The battle, and the victory, lies not only with the champion athlete, but with those good athletes in the middle, those for whom training and sacrifice may be just as important as for the elite, but more difficult as the rewards may be less tangible and the questions and self-doubts greater. And it is a ripple effect. The battle and the victory are issues for the beginning runner as well.

Janet Guthrie, the first woman driver to qualify for the Indianapolis 500, thanked her parents "for not bringing me up thinking I couldn't do something because I was a woman." Future success lies in maximizing human potential, in eradicating the lies and limitations that lessen our self-worth. We must cultivate ambition and determination, and develop the necessary resilience to persevere.

Although it's a start, a real revolution will take more than having eight thousand entrants on the starting line of an all-women's race. As long as there are rules and limitations dictated by others in power, it will take constant struggle to gain control of our own destiny.

A woman runner should know what that takes. Whether it's just making the time to get out the door for a run, finishing a marathon, or finding a way to run against all odds, she should understand the guts and drive needed to make a real revolution, and make it work.

We must become, and remain, the makers of a revolution—a fight for the right to make our own choices and decisions. This revolution, like all struggles from which we achieve growth, will not be without its risks. We must remember the courage, keep alive the anger, flaunt our pride, and be confident of what we can become. No matter what the gains, we must continue. Our reach must forever exceed our grasp.

Appendices

Survey 1983
L'eggs Mini Marathon
New York Road Runners Club

ternational   Running   Center
East 89th Street
ew York, NY 10028
212) 860-4455

Mailing   Address:
P.O. Box 881, FDR Station
New York, NY 10150

Telex
238093 NYRR UR

Attention
WOMEN RUNNERS

his is a survey for a book on women as runners and athletes—a book for you! The
Jew York Runners Club would like your thoughts. Please take a minute to fill out this
urvey, and give it in at the lobby of the International Running Center. THANKS!

Vhat is your age? _____

Vhere are you from? _____

low long have you been running? _____

low much do you run a week (miles)? _____

Are you on a running team? Yes _____   No _____

Do you have a coach? Yes _____   No _____

Vhen did you begin racing? _____

low many times a year do you race? _____

Vhat distances? _____

Do you participate in other sports? Yes _____   No _____

Did you participate in other sports before you began to run? Yes _____   No _____

Do you usually run alone? Always _____   Never _____   Sometimes _____

Do you usually run with other women? Always _____   Never _____   Sometimes _____

Do you usually run with men? Always _____   Never _____   Sometimes _____

Do you run a combination of some, or all of the above?

Always _____   Never _____   Sometimes _____

Do you consider yourself an athlete? Yes _____   No _____

Have you always considered yourself an athlete? Yes _____   No _____

175

Number in order of importance topics you'd like to know more about, with 1 (highest) to 7 (lowest, or least important).

History of women's running, and struggle for current status   #1-7 _____

Medical aspects of women's running   #1-7 _____

Coaching for women   #1-7 _____

Profiles on top women runners   #1-7 _____

Profiles on recreational women runners   #1-7 _____

Running for your daughters, or young girls   #1-7 _____

Sociological/psychological significance of women's running   #1-7 _____

What is the greatest benefit of being a woman runner?

What, if any, is, or was, your biggest concern about being a woman runner?

YOUR FEELINGS?   YOUR OPINION?   YOUR EXPERIENCES?

If there is anything you are willing to share which you could take time to add, it would be very useful, and greatly appreciated.

L'eggs Mini Marathon May 28, 1983
DEMOGRAPHICS ON ENTRANTS

Total Runners by Age Group

15 and under	207
16-19	253
20-29	2382
30-39	2264
40-49	633
50-59	135
60-69	23
70 and over	2
Total Entrants	5899
Youngest Runner	6
Oldest Runner	72

Totals by Best Previous Time

30:01-35:00	43
35:01-40:00	116
40:01-45:00	365
45:01-50:00	824
50:01-55:00	873
55:01-1:00:00	882
1:00:01-1:05:00	364
1:05:01-1:10:00	210
1:10:01-1:15:00	103
1:15:01-1:20:00	51
1:20:00 or slower	78
No Response	1990

Totals by Predicted Time

30:01-35:00	31
35:01-40:00	166
40:01-45:00	430
45:01-50:00	1020
50:01-55:00	840
55:01-1:00:00	1131
1:00:01-1:05:00	217
1:05:01-1:10:00	206
1:10:01-1:15:00	110
1:15:01-1:20:00	56
1:20:00 and slower	110
No Response	1582

Totals by NYRRC Membership

NYRRC Members	1976
Non-members	3923
Total	5899

Totals by Occupation

Accountant	83
Actuary	9
Administrator/Manager	250
Airplane Pilot	3
Architect	16
Artist	131
Attorney/Lawyer	108
Banker	107
Bartender	7
Beautician/Hairdresser	7
Builder	0
Business Owner	28
Chairman/Pres. of Co.	2
Chef/Cook/Baker	14
Civil Servant	39
Clergy	3
Clerical	63
Computer Programmer/Analyst	84
Construction Occupation	4
Communications	60
Consultant	65
Craftsperson	12
Counselor	34
Data Processing	57
Designer	60
Dental Asst./Lab Technician	25
Dentist	7
Driver (Truck, Cab)	5
Economist	7
Editor	70
Engineer	24
Electrician	0
Federal Agent	3
Filmmaker	9
Financial Analyst	56
Fire Fighter	3
Flight Attendant	39
Gamekeeper/Forest Service	5
Health Related Occupation	125
Homemaker	304
Investment Broker	15
Insurance Agent/Broker	23
International Occupation	8
Laborer	0
Librarian	24
Machinist	0
Manufacturer	4
Marketing	74
Mathematician	6

Musician	40	W. Germany	3
Mechanic	1	Alabama	0
Newsperson	10	Alaska	0
Nurse	298	Arizona	2
Nutritionist	24	Arkansas	2
Performing Artist	57	California	16
Pharmacist	4	Colorado	5
Photographer	15	Connecticut	188
Physical Therapist	26	Delaware	7
Physician/Doctor	43	District of Columbia	7
Police/Law Enforcement	23	Florida	15
Politician	3	Georgia	4
Postal Employee	12	Hawaii	3
Printer/Pressman	4	Idaho	0
Psychologist	49	Illinois	10
Psychotherapist	24	Indiana	6
Production Person	18	Iowa	0
Publisher	26	Kansas	0
Public Relations	42	Kentucky	0
Radio/TV	33	Louisiana	2
Real Estate Agent	16	Maine	3
Recreation Worker	29	Maryland	30
Research Analyst	34	Massachusetts	109
Retail Trade Occupation	39	Michigan	5
Retired	7	Minnesota	3
Sales Manager	30	Mississippi	0
Scientist	44	Missouri	0
Salesperson	87	Montana	0
Secretary	295	Nebraska	2
Security Guard	2	Nevada	1
Social Worker	118	New Hampshire	13
Stockbroker	7	New Jersey	715
Student	777	New Mexico	1
Systems Analyst	29	New York	4516
Teacher/Educator	583	North Carolina	10
Unemployed	32	North Dakota	0
US Military Services	4	Ohio	21
Urban Planner	9	Oklahoma	0
Waiter/Waitress	27	Oregon	0
Wall Street Occupation	31	Pennsylvania	117
Writer/Journalist	88	Rhode Island	16
Other	777	South Carolina	0
		South Dakota	0
		Tennessee	1

Totals by State and Country

		Texas	6
		Utah	1
Bermuda	3	Vermont	11
Brazil	3	Virginia	28
Canada	7	Washington	1
Ireland	2	West Virginia	0
Mexico	1	Wisconsin	1
N. Ireland	1	Wyoming	0
Norway	1	Unknown	24

Results of the 1983 L'eggs Mini Marathon Survey

T HE L'EGGS MINI MARATHON in Central Park is a springtime celebration of women's running by over six thousand participants. But more, it is a statement of emergence—a day and a place to show who women runners are and what they can do.

A total of 930 women in the 1983 L'eggs Mini Marathon completed this survey. Every type of woman filled out the questionnaire, from the winner of the race, Anne Audain, to the novice completing her first 10-kilometer. The number of respondents for different questions will not always total 930 because not all the women answered all the questions. (For example, of the 930 women, the mean age of 31.4 years is based on 925 respondents.) Each item will include the total number of women who responded to that particular question, indicated by the letter *N*.

RESPONDENTS AS A WHOLE

The mean age of the total sample is 31.4 years (*N* = 925). As a point of reference, this compares to the mean age of women in the 1983 New York City Marathon, 34 years (*N* = 2,850) and 33 years for New York Road Runners Club women members (*N* = 6,753). The following table gives age breakdowns for the survey. The largest age group, 30 to 39, represents 40.4 percent of the sample. The same age group represents 43.2 percent of the participants in the 1983 New York City Marathon and 44 percent of the NYRRC membership.

19 or under	26 (2.8%)
20 to 24	130 (14.1%)
25 to 29	274 (29.6%)
30 to 34	210 (22.7%)
35 to 39	164 (17.7%)
40 to 44	62 (6.7%)
45 to 49	34 (3.7%)
50 to 54	14 (1.5%)
55 to 59	7 (0.8%)
60 or over	4 (0.4%)

These women have been running an average of 46.9 months, or just under four years ($N = 916$). They report that they run an average of 23.4 miles per week ($N = 903$), that they enter 7.8 races in a year ($N = 753$) with the average race distance 7.5 miles ($N = 799$). There is an obvious peculiarity about the last two numbers. Only 753 women report how many races they run a year, but more than that number (799) report what distances they race. For many of these women this was their first race (40 percent of all L'eggs entrants are running their first race) and therefore the question "How many times a year do you race?" is meaningless, so this question was counted as missing data. The reason that the N for the question on race distances is higher is that some of the women put down the distance of the Mini, and when they did their answers were not included in the analysis.

RESPONDENTS BY CATEGORY

The women were separated into categories based on the miles they ran per week and the number of races they ran per year. Women who ran under 40 miles or entered fewer than 10 races per year were given the category "Less Serious;" those who ran over 40 miles per week and 10 or more races per year were classified as "Serious," and those running over 60 miles per week were designated "Elite." The total for "Serious" is 58 and for "Elite" 18.

Serious versus Less Serious

	Serious		Less Serious	
	N	Mean	N	Mean
Age	58	31.6	867	31.4
How long running?	58	74.1 months (6.2 years)	858	45.1 months (3.8 years)
Miles run/week?	58	54.8	845	21.2
Number races/year?	58	20.2	695	6.7
Distance of race?	58	11.9 miles	741	7.1 miles

The statistician, a Columbia University psychologist, pointed out the significant difference in these numbers. One hundred percent of the Serious group answered every question for which data were recorded. The consistency (58, 58, 58 . . .) is quite remarkable. However, there is more than one way of interpreting this phenomenon. Several possible causes can be attributed, but they are merely speculations. The statistician reports the following. "If we begin with the naive assumption that there is something a little more competent about simply being able to complete a task such as filling out a questionnaire with no problems, we might suspect one of two things: the causality is in the direction *running => competence*, that is, engaging in that sort of physical exercise on a daily basis affects one in such a way that the individual deals more ably with certain types of situations. It sounds a little farfetched, but the concept is just a restatement of the old 'sound body leads to sound mind.' It is considerably more likely, however, that there is a selection process operating. That is, the type of person who displays the one behavior (running 40 miles per week) is more likely to display competence, if that is what it is, in other areas. If one continued to theorize along these lines, the notions of self-concept, self-respect, etc., would probably be the focus. Of course, 'competence' need not be the basis on which these individuals are selected. It could equally well be compulsivity or even obsessiveness. And of course a million different things could account for the relationships. It may be, for example, that the Serious runners build up more, or maybe even less, arousal (adrenaline, etc.) before the race, and this increased/decreased arousal level interferes (in the case of the Less Serious group) or facilitates (in the case of the Serious group) the behavior." It could also be that greater interest in the subject would lead to greater responsiveness.

As for the other comparisons between the two groups, the age is the same for both. Not surprisingly, the Serious group has been running quite a bit longer (6.2 versus 3.8 years). The difference in miles is obvious as the groups were broken down on that basis. The same is true for the number of races per year.

Elite versus Non-Elite Elite is defined as those women who run 60 or more miles per week and at least 10 races per year. In the following table, the Non-Elite group listed does includes some of the women who are also included in the Serious group, and the women in the Elite group are of course also all members of the Serious group.

	Elite		Non-Elite	
	N	Mean	N	Mean
Age	18	27.7	907	31.5
How long running?	18	85.1 months	898	46.1 months
		(7.1 years)		(3.8 years)
Miles run/week?	18	76.0	885	22.3
Number races/year?	18	20.7	735	7.4
Distance of race?	18	10.8 miles	781	7.4 miles

In the Elite group, the mean age finally drops, indicating a fundamental difference about the 60-plus-mile group. Several speculations can be derived from this fact. Perhaps the Elite group had greater opportunities and a more serious background, as seven years of running means most of them began in college where they may have run competitively. The Less Serious began in their mid- to late 20s—before the running boom, when the emphasis in college was on politics, not sports—and therefore probably began running well after college for fitness and/or social reasons. So "Elite" may reflect opportunity and timing at least as much as talent. On the other hand, the Elite group did not begin running before college age, and if this study were done ten years from now, the number of years of running (and possibly the achievements) may be even greater for the Elite group, as high school running did not really get under way until Title IX in the mid-seventies. More miles (i.e., more seriousness) may also reflect the Elite group having or making more time to train than the Non-Elite. A woman who began running pre-career and/or family has learned to make time for her running, a habit she began in college.

Although the number of races is greater for the Elite group, both groups are racing 5 percent of their total training mileage, indicating that at both levels runners are training/racing in a proper ratio, based on the assumption of course that the Elite know what they are doing. The race distance average is only slightly higher, since the distance of the race is not as important as how seriously it is run. The Elite runners are probably more selective of their races because a race takes more out of them: they are more competitive, thus under greater pressure, and with more at stake than the other runners. Many of the Elite are career runners, and they can run only so many races without burning out.

Summary of Basic Statistics

	Total	Serious	Elite
Age	31.4 (925)	31.6 (58)	27.7 (18)
How long running? (years)	3.9 (916)	6.2 (58)	7.1 (18)
Miles run/week?	23.4 (903)	54.8 (58)	76.0 (18)
Number races/year?	7.8 (753)	20.2 (58)	20.7 (18)
Distance of race?	7.5 (799)	11.9 (58)	10.8 (18)

PREFERENCES AND SELF-IMAGE

The tallies below are for the following questions:
1. Do you usually run alone? (abbreviated "Alone?")
2. Do you usually run with other women? ("W/Women?")
3. Do you usually run with men? ("W/Men?")
4. Do you consider yourself an athlete? ("Athlete?")
5. The topic of interest rated number one ("Topic").

The tallies for the first four questions are broken down by Total, Serious, Less Serious, and Elite Non-Elite.

TOTAL

	Always	Never	Sometimes
Alone?	365 (39.7%)	26 (2.8%)	528 (57.4%)
W/Women?	46 (5.1%)	241 (26.9%)	610 (68.0%)
W/Men?	46 (5.2%)	212 (23.7%)	635 (71.1%)

	Yes	No
Athlete?	648 (71.9%)	248 (27.5%)

Topic	
Medical aspects of women's running	355 (51.5%)
Sociological/psychological	97 (14.1%)
Coaching for women	85 (12.3%)
History of women's running	61 (8.9%)
Running for daughters, young girls	37 (5.4%)
Profiles on recreational runners	25 (3.6%)
Profiles on top women runners	22 (3.2%)

Percentages will not always add to 100 because of missing data.

SERIOUS

	Always	Never	Sometimes
Alone?	17 (28.8%)	1 (1.8%)	39 (68.4%)
W/Women?	2 (3.5%)	13 (22.8%)	42 (73.7%)
W/Men?	8 (14.0%)	8 (14.0%)	41 (71.9%)

	Yes	No
Athlete?	51 (91.1%)	5 (8.9%)

Topic	
Medical aspects of women's running	16 (35.6%)
Coaching for women	9 (20.0%)
Profiles on top women runners	7 (15.6%)
Sociological/psychological	6 (13.3%)
History of women's running	4 (8.9%)
Running for daughters, young girls	2 (4.4%)
Profiles on recreational runners	1 (2.2%)

The Serious group is, not surprisingly, more interested in coaching for women, ranking it number two. For the rest, however, there are no significant differences. Most respondents voted medical aspects as their first preference.

Data for the Less Serious group are presented below for comparison.

LESS SERIOUS

	Always	Never	Sometimes
Alone?	348 (40.3%)	25 (2.9%)	489 (56.6%)
W/Women?	44 (5.2%)	228 (27.1%)	568 (67.6%)
W/Men?	38 (4.5%)	204 (24.2%)	594 (71.1%)

	Yes	No
Athlete?	597 (70.7%)	243 (28.8%)

Notice the contrast of this group classifying themselves as nonathletes (28.8%) with the percentage for the Serious group (8.9%).

ELITE

	Always	Never	Sometimes
Alone?	2 (11.1%)	0 (0.0%)	16 (88.9%)
W/Women?	1 (5.6%)	2 (11.1%)	15 (83.3%)
W/Men?	5 (27.8%)	1 (5.6%)	12 (66.7%)

	Yes	No
Athlete?	16 (100%)	0

The following data for the Non-Elite group are presented for comparison.

	Always	Never	Sometimes
Alone?	363 (40.2%)	26 (2.9%)	512 (56.8%)
W/Women?	45 (5.1%)	239 (27.2%)	595 (67.7%)
W/Men?	41 (4.7%)	211 (24.1%)	623 (71.2%)

	Yes	No
Athlete?	632 (71.4%)	248 (28.0%)

Notice that the elite woman trains more with men, and never trains all the time by herself. This is probably a result of the type of training she is doing, which necessitates she train with faster runners to motivate herself to push harder. Because she is elite among women, these partners are usually men unless she is on a team or in a group of her peers. Running which serves as meditation or relaxation in which one is not required to push beyond one's limits or to concentrate on the task of running hard can more easily be done alone (hence the results for the other groups), whereas it is much more difficult for an elite runner to follow a training program without training partners.

A summary table follows for the question, "Do you consider yourself an athlete?"

Yes	No		Yes	No
			Total	
			648 (71.9%)	248 (27.5%)
Serious			**Less-Serious**	
51 (91.1%)	5 (8.9%)		597 (70.7%)	243 (28.8%)
Elite			**Non-Elite**	
16 (100%)	0		632 (71.4%)	248 (28.0%)

Nine percent of the women in the Serious group still fail to classify themselves as athletes. Although this is not a remarkably high percentage, it is still interesting to speculate why a woman who runs 40-plus miles a week and races at least 10 races a year would not consider herself an athlete. Perhaps it indicates a lack of complete identification by these women as to who they are and what they do. They may consider being an athlete out of their range, when in fact their lifestyles (e.g., running 40 miles per week) do in fact belong to athletes.

FEELINGS, OPINIONS, AND EXPERIENCES

The comments section included several typical responses for the three questions, which are listed below.

- *What is the greatest benefit of being a woman runner?*

Feeling good about myself; sense of accomplishment; knowing I can do it; self-confidence; respect from others; self-esteem; gaining control; keeping weight down; being fit; coping with stress; increased psychological and physical well-being.

Some individual responses to this question:
"Not feeling like a helpless female"; "strength"; "opportunity to be openly competitive"; "the ability to do something for and by my-self"; "increased self-confidence in other areas of my life." "The greatest benefit of being a woman runner is being a woman and showing men even though we aren't always as strong that we are still dedicated" (from a 14-year-old!).

• *What, if any, is, or was, your biggest concern about being a woman runner?*
The overwhelming majority of women wrote SAFETY; verbal abuse; attack; rape. The second-greatest response was medical/physical ef-fects (in order of frequency): effect on body in general; breasts; child-bearing; knees and skin; self-consciousness about the way they looked when running; fear of lack of stick-to-itiveness.

Some individual responses to this question:
"Looking clumsy"; "Does running cause breast cancer?"; "Does run-ning cause the breasts to sag?"; "I have heard that running is bad for your face, causing it to sag!!"; "When I started running, few women ran, so I was told I would get hair on my chest, a low husky voice, and stringy muscles. That was a big concern because I had no other women runners to compare myself to. But on the contrary, running makes me more of a woman."

• *Your Feelings?*   *Your Opinion?*   *Your Experiences?*
"My dearest friend took up running with me less than a year ago. Prior to that her most strenuous activity was the daily application of eyeshadow."

"I'd like to see the day when 'women's running' can be talked about as 'running.'"

"Running is a great antidote to the claustrophobia of motherhood."

"There are days when I feel that running was a gift to me, irrational though that sounds—that it was suddenly presented to me when life had gotten toughest, to enable me to cope. More experienced runners have (condescendingly) commented that this is a typical syndrome for the beginner runner. 'It's like a love affair the first couple of years, then you get it into perspective.' Maybe. But it has become so important to me in terms of maintaining my balance, providing insight, permitting me to be alone (and comfortable) with myself, that I rarely reveal to anyone how important it is to me for fear of being laughed at or of baring a critical vulnerability.''

Resource List

MAGAZINES

The International Running Center Library at the New York Road Runners Club, 9 East 89th Street, New York, New York 10128, (212) 860-4455, subscribes to all of the following publications as well as to many regional running magazines and club newsletters. In addition to its present book collection (all those listed here are included) of over four hundred volumes, the library has a number of films and video cassettes on races and running-related subjects. All materials in the library are for on-site research, although the librarian will gladly respond to written inquiries when possible. Send self-addressed, stamped envelope (SASE).

United States

Footnotes
RRCA Newsletter
11155 Saffold Way
Reston, VA 22090
(703) 437-8586

Master Runner
210 7th St. SE
Suite C-23
Washington, DC 20003
(202) 546-5598

The Physician and Sports Medicine
4530 W. 77th St.
Minneapolis, MN 55435
(612) 835-3222

Road Race Management
14416 Jefferson Davis Highway
Woodbridge, VA 22191
(703) 491-2044

The Runner
One Park Avenue
New York, NY 10016
(212) 725-3500

Running Advice
576 Armour Circle
Atlanta, GA 30324
(800) 241-4603
(404) 892-1158

Running Commentary
130 East 34th Place
Eugene, OR 97405
(505) 683-2118

Running Times
14416 Jefferson Davis Highway
Woodbridge, VA 22191
(703) 491-2044

Runner's World
1400 Stierlin Rd
Mountain View, CA 94043
(415) 965-8777

Track & Field News
Box 296
Los Altos, CA 94022
(415) 948-8188

Tri-Athlete
6660 Banning Dr.
Oakland, CA 94611
(415) 530-4580

Triathlon
PO Box 5901
Santa Monica, CA 90405
(213) 558-3321

Ultrarunning
PO Box 1057
Amherst, MA 01002
(413) 549-2838

Women's Sports
310 Town & Country Village
Palo Alto, CA 94301
(415) 321-5102

Women's Track & Field World
PO Box 371
Claremont, CA 91711
(714) 624-5955

England

Athletics Weekly
342 High St.
Rochester, Kent
England
(0634) 409260

British Journal of Sports Medicine
39 Linkfield Rd.
Mountsorrel, Loughborough
Leicestershire, England

*International Amateur Athletic
Federation Bulletin*
3 Hans Crescent
Knightsbridge
London SW England
01-581 8771

Running
57-61 Mortimer St.
London, W 1N 7TD
England
01-637-4383

Running Review
2 Tower St.
Hyde, Cheshire
England
061-366-9732

France

Courir
1 Allée Des Myosotis
Saint Denis 93200
France
524 40 59

Jogging International
50 Rue Du Faubourg-Du-Temple
Paris, France
206 15 57

Italy

Correre
Via V. Monti 12
20123 Milano
Italy
876547/803496

Ireland

Irish Runner
Athletic Publishing Ltd.
PO Box 1227
Dublin 8 Ireland
698331

Netherlands

European Runners
Postbus 221
Valkenburg Geul 6300
Netherlands
04406-14646

West Germany

Leicht Athletik
Postfach 650380
D 1000 Berlin
West Germany
(030) 461 10 11

Spiridon
Poststr 40 4010
Hilden, West Germany
021 03/ 542 78

New Zealand

New Zealand Runner
Box 29-043
Auckland, New Zealand
797-341/342

Australia

Australian Runner
Box 396
South Yarra 3141
Australia
(03) 209 9197

Portugal

Spiridon
Redacco: Av Do Uruguai
Lisbon 4, Portugal
711487

Switzerland

Spiridon
1922 Salvan
Suisse
(026) 6 12 12

Norway

Kondis
Postboks 1009
Tromso, Norway
2 05 08 21

Belgium

Loop
Postbus 7
Brugge 1 B-8000
Belgium
(050) 33.37.67

Denmark

Atletik NYT
Bispebjerg Park Alle 27
Copenhagen, Denmark
(01) 838891 (20-22)

South Africa

S.A. Runner
8 Savell Ave.
Glenashley 4051
South Africa
(031) 52-3568

Canada

Canadian Runner
23 Brentcliffe Rd.
Toronto, M464 B 7
Canada
(416) 425-6699

Canadian Track & Field
355 River Rd.
Vanier City
Ontario K1L8C1, Canada
(613) 744-1160

Japan

Runners
2-6-1 Tomigaya
Shibuya-Ku, Tokyo 151, Japan

Spain

Marathon
Jonqueres 16 9-C
Barcelona 3, Spain
301 12 30

Sweden

Jogging
Box 10023
S-100 Stockholm
Sweden
08-61 6721

China

China Sports
8 Tiyuguan Rd.
Beijing, China

U.S.S.R.

Sport in the U.S.S.R.
Mezhdunarodnaya Kniga
Moscow 6-200
U.S.S.R.

Finland

Juoksija
Formaalintie
Juoksijalehti
20780 Kaarina
Finland

Brazil

A Corrida
Rua Da Laranjeiras 363
Rio De Janeiro 22240
Brazil

BOOKS

Fitness, General

Cooper, Kenneth H., and Mildred Bantam, 1973 — *Aerobics for Women*

Rosenzweig, Sandra Harper & Row, 1982 — *Sports Fitness for Women*

Guides

Hayes, Aden, and Jere Van Dyk Penguin, 1980 — *A Runner's Guide to Europe*

Scheerer, P., and J. Schwanbeck Dutton, 1979 — *The Traveling Runner's Guide*

Temple, Cliff Tantivy Press Ltd., 1983 — *International Running Guide*

Running, General

Fixx, Jim Random House, 1979 — *The Complete Book of Running*

Glover, Bob, and Jack Shepherd Penguin, 1978 — *The Runner's Handbook*

Henderson, Joe
World Publications, 1977
Jog, Run, Race

Runners World, Editors of
World Publications, 1978
The Complete Runner

Sports Medicine

Marshall, John L., M.D., with
Heather Barbash
Delacorte Press, 1981
The Sports Doctor's Fitness Book for Women

Shangold, Mona, M.D., and Gabe
Mirkin, M.D.
Simon & Schuster (planned publication in 1984)
The Complete Sportsmedicine Book for Women

Sheehan, George, M.D.
World Publications, 1981
Medical Advice for Runners

Southmayd, W., and M. Hoffman
Quick Fox, 1981
Sports Health: Book of Athletic Injuries

Women

Boutilier, Mary A., and Lucinda
San Giovanni
Human Kinetics, 1983
The Sporting Woman

Runner's World, Editors of
World Publications, 1978
The Complete Woman Runner

Squires, Bill, and Raymond Krise
Stephen Greene Press, 1983
Improving Women's Running

Ullyot, Joan L., M.D.
Putnam, 1980
Running Free

Ullyot, Joan L., M.D.
World Publications, 1976
Women's Running

Training & Competition

A number of good books on this subject have been written by the following: Bill Dellinger, Bob Glover & Peter Schuder, Marty Liquori, Arthur Lydiard, *Runner's World,* Bill Squires, *Track & Field News.*

ORGANIZATIONS

President's Council on Physical Fitness
Suite 7103
450 5th Street, N.W.
Washington, DC
(202) 272-3421

American Running & Fitness Association
2420 K St., N.W.
Washington, DC 20037
(202) 965-3430

A national organization of individual members. Send SASE for information on membership dues, fitness programs, and quarterly newsletter. Send SASE for current nationwide directory and survey of sportsmedicine clinics.

Road Runners Club of America
8811 Edgehill Drive
Huntsville, AL 35802
(205) 881-9077

A national organization of 408 chapter clubs covering 47 states and representing nearly 100,000 members. RRCA clubs put on thousands of races every year; send SASE for current chapter list to locate an RRCA club in your area. RRCA publishes *Footnotes*, a quarterly newspaper with feature articles and other information (see "Magazines").

RRCA also sponsors a Personal Fitness Program aimed at the noncompetitive runner. Send SASE for information to: Paul W. Hronjak, 627 N. Jameson Ave., Lima, OH 45805, or call (419) 225-9777.

The Athletics Congress (TAC)
PO Box 120
Indianapolis, IN 46206
(317) 638-9155

National governing body for athletics (track and field and road running in the United States). Send SASE for directory of local/regional TAC chapters and information on the following committees dealing specifically with women's issues.

Women's Development Committee
c/o Dr. Harmon Brown
345 Bowfin
Foster City
CA 94404

and Committee on Long Distance Running/Women
c/o Nina Kuscsik
7 Flint Court
Huntington Station, NY
11746

International Amateur Athletic Federation (IAAF)
3 Hans Crescent
Knightsbridge, London SW
England
01-581 8771/2/3/4

International organization governing international amateur athletic competition. IAAF publishes a quarterly bulletin and other informational material.

National Running Data Center
PO Box 42888
Tucson, AZ 85733
(602) 326-6416

National statistics keeper. Publishes: running records by age, in-depth masters rankings, certified courses, U.S. rankings annually, and the NRDC monthly newsletter.

National Collegiate Athletic Association (NCAA)
US Highway 50 & Nall Ave.
Box 1906
Shawnee Mission, KS 66222
(913) 384-3220

Governs athletic competition for member colleges and universities.

Women's Sports Foundation
195 Moulton St.
San Francisco, CA 94123
(800) 227-3988

New York Road Runners Club
9 East 89th Street
New York, NY 10128
(212) 860-4455

Largest running club in the world; conducts the New York City Marathon, the L'eggs Mini Marathon, the Fifth Avenue Mile and 200 races at varying distances throughout the year; sponsors many running-related clinics and publishes *New York Running News.* The club is located at the International Running Center in New York and houses the Albert H. Gordon International Running Library and research center. Send SASE for membership, calendar, and race information.

Association of Road Racing Athletes
1460 Paulsen Bldg.
Spokane, WA 99205
(509) 328-9048

An organization which has geared its efforts toward the concept of open competition and prize money events. ARRA sponsors a race circuit and other related events. Send SASE for membership and race circuit information.

International Runners' Committee
2011 Kimberly Drive
Eugene, OR 97405

An organization whose initial objective has been to secure a program of distance races for women in the Olympics. Additional goals include world road racing championships, acceptance of world road race records, and expansion of competitive opportunities for men and women worldwide.

Association of International Marathons
PO Box 10-106
Hamilton, New Zealand
(71) 493-369

An organization of over 45 international marathon directors working on exchange of technical information and coordination of marathon schedules. Send SASE for membership and race calendar information.

Avon International Running Circuit
9 West 57th Street
New York, NY 10019
(212) 546-6070

Send SASE for information on national and international race circuit and for Avon's "Marathon Training Tips" booklet.

L'eggs Mini Marathon
c/o New York Road Runners Club
9 East 89th St.
New York, NY 10128
(212) 860-4455

Send SASE for information on the most prestigious all-women's 10-kilometer race in the world.

Bonne Bell 10 Kilometer Race Series
Georgetown Row
Lakewood, OH 44107
(216) 221-0800

Send SASE for information on road race circuit as well as all-women's triathlons.

Women on the Run Race Series
25 E. Court St.
Greenville, SC 29601
(803) 242-6300

Send SASE for information on nationwide road races and all-women's triathlons.

Women's Distance Festival Race Series
c/o Road Runners Club of America
8811 Edgehill Drive
Huntsville, AL 35802
(205) 881-9077

Send SASE for information race dates and participating clubs.

Colgate Women's Games
300 Park Avenue
New York, NY 10022
(212) 310-2000

Largest all-women's track meet in the world. Send SASE for information.

Evening Press/Brooks Women's Mini Marathon
c/o The Dundrum Athletic Club
O'Connell St.
Dublin 2, Ireland

Send SASE for information on this international all-women's 10-kilometer race. Over 8,000 participated in its first running in 1983.

Moving Comfort Women's Running Series
5412 Eisenhower Avenue
Alexandria, VA 22304
(703) 823-5555

Send SASE for information and race calendar.

9 West Women's 4 Mile Runs
c/o Booke & Co.
355 Lexington Avenue
New York, NY 10017
(212) 490-9095

Send SASE for information and race calendar.

AVAILABLE MEDICAL HELP

American Massage Therapy Association
P.O. Box 1270
Kingsport, TN 37662
(615) 245-8071

American Chiropractic Association
Council on Sports Injuries and Physical Fitness
also
Council on Orthopedics
1916 Wilson Blvd.
Arlington, VA 22201
(703) 276-8800

Institute for Physical Fitness and Myotherapy*
PO Box 625
Stockbridge, MA 01262
(413) 298-3066

* (myo = muscle; therapy = service to)

American Anorexia/Bulimia Association, Inc.
133 Cedar Lane
Teaneck, NJ 07666
(201) 836-1800

F.A.R.E. (Foundation for Athletic Research and Education)
Dr. Leroy Perry
3283 Motor Avenue
West Los Angeles, CA 90034
(213) 555-6900

American College of Obstetricians & Gynecologists
600 Maryland Avenue, S.W.
Washington, DC
(202) 638-5577

Send SASE for planned nationwide directory and survey of sportsmedicine clinics.

Sports Gynecology Center
New York Hospital/Cornell Medical Center
525 East 68th Street
New York, NY 10022
(212) 472-5454

Melpomene Institute
316 Universey Avenue
St. Paul, MN 55103
(612) 646-2252 or 822-1661

Nonprofit agency disseminating information on physically active women.

American College of Sports Medicine
1 Virginia Ave., Suite 340
PO Box 1440
Indianapolis, IN 46206
(317) 637-9200

Disseminates information to those in the medical profession as well as to the public; publishes a monthly bulletin and an annual directory of members; conducts conferences and issues position statements regarding effects of exercise and sports.

American Medical Joggers Association
Box 4704
North Hollywood, CA 91607
(213) 989-3432

Conducts and sponsors medical symposia; publishes a monthly
newsletter; membership comprised of doctors and health professionals.

BIBLIOGRAPHY

PART I: THE WOMAN ATHLETE

Aigner, Hal. "Why Sports Get You High." *Women's Sports,* December 1974.

Andrews, Valerie. "Do Marriage and Mileage Mix?" *The Runner,* September 1980.

"Athletic Supporters." *Women's Sports,* May 1981.

Averbuch, Gloria. "Age of Athletics." *New York Running News,* August/September 1983.

———. "The American Odyssey." *New York Running News,* October 1980.

———. "Second Hand Rosie." *New York Running News,* June/July 1980.

Ayres, Alex. "Will Running Change the Kind of Person You Are?" *Running Times,* September 1982.

Benoit, Joan. "The Female Elite—Training for the '80's." *New York Running News,* October 24, 1982.

Boutilier, Mary A., and Lucinda San Giovanni. *The Sporting Woman.* Champaign, IL: Human Kinetics Publishers, 1983.

Bunker Rohrbaugh, Joanna. "Femininity on the Line." *Psychology Today,* August 1979.

Campbell, Candace. "Joyce Smith." *Master Runner,* October 1983.

Chester, David. *Olympic Games Handbook.* New York: Charles Scribner's Sons, 1975.

The Complete Woman Runner. Mountain View, CA: World Publications, 1978.

A Comprehensive Report on Women's Long Distance Running. New York: Avon Products, Inc., Fourth Printing, 1981.

Costill, David, L., Ph.D. *A Scientific Approach to Distance Running.* Tafnews Press, 1979.

"A Drift of Fine Woman." *Irish Runner*, vol. 3, no. 5, August 1983.

Elkins, Hollis. "Time for a Change: Women's Athletics and the Women's Movement." *Frontiers*, vol. 3, no. 1, Spring 1978.

"Female Runners File Suit." *The New York Times*, August 12, 1983.

Goodman, Mark. "Women on the Run." *The New York Times Magazine*, August 7, 1983.

Grossman, Ellie. *In Her 60's, This Lady Became a Jogger.* New York: Newspaper Enterprise Association, July 11, 1983.

Harris, Dorothy V. "Female Sport Today: Psychological Considerations." *International Journal of Sports Psychology*, vol. 10, 1979.

Harris, Mary B. "Women Runners' Views of Running." *Perceptual and Motor Skills*, 1981.

"Iron Deficiency in Adolescent Cross-Country Runners." *The Physician and Sports Medicine*, vol. 2, no. 6, June 1983.

"Is Running for Children?" *The Health Letter*, May 27, 1983.

Jackman, Phil. "The Marathon Woman." *The Los Angeles Times*, May 8, 1983.

"Joan Benoit Sets World Mark." *The New York Times*, April 19, 1983.

Kellogg, Rick. "Mary Decker Tabb's Endless Summer." *The New York Times*, July 25, 1982.

Krise, Raymond, and Bill Squires. *Fast Tracks: The History of Distance Running.* Brattleboro, VT: The Stephen Greene Press, 1982.

Lyle, Candace. "A Long Distance Original." *The Runner*, May 1983.

Lorway, Jon. "The Liberty Athletic Club in Pursuit of Excellence." *Boston Running News*, September/October 1983.

"Make Way for the New Spartans." *Time*, September 19, 1983.

"The Making of America's Best." *Newsweek*, August 15, 1983.

"Master Profile—Cindy Dalrymple." *Master Runner*, April 1983.

Miller Lite Report on American Attitudes Toward Sports. Milwaukee, Wisconsin: Miller Brewing Co., 1983.

Moore, Kenny and Lisa Twyman. "The Marathon's Maine Woman." *Sports Illustrated*, April 1983.

"The New Ideal of Beauty." *Time*, August 30, 1982.

Nickerson, H. James, M.D., and Alan D. Tripp, M.S. "Iron Deficiency in Adolescent Cross-Country Runners." *The Physician and Sports Medicine*, vol. 2, no. 6, June 1983.

"1982 Women's World Rankings." *Track and Field News*, December 1982.

Olsen, Eric. "Kid Stuff." *The Runner*, November 1982.

———. "Mary Decker: At the Crossroads." *The Runner*, January 1980.

"On the Road." *Track and Field News*, October 1983.

Parkhouse, Bonnie L., and Jackie Lapin. *Women Who Win: Exercising Your*

Rights in Sports. Englewood Cliffs, New Jersey: Prentice-Hall, Inc., 1980.

"The Running Nun." *The New York Times,* December 11, 1983.

Sacks, Michael H., M.D., ed., and Michael L. Sachs, Ph.D., assoc. ed. *Psychology of Running.* Champaign, IL: Human Kinetics Publishers, Inc., 1981.

Schreiber, Linda. "Running Through Divorce: The Ups and Downs." *New York Running News,* August/September 1983.

Shangold, Mona, M.D. "Running for Young Girls." *Running New Jersey,* March 1983.

———. "Women's Running." *Runner's World,* August 1982.

Sheehan, George, M.D. *This Running Life.* New York: Simon and Schuster, 1980.

Slater, Chuck. "Ron Tabb's Achieving a Singular Success." *The New York Daily News,* October 16, 1983.

Talamini, John T., and Charles H. Page. *Sports and Society.* Toronto: Little, Brown & Co., 1973.

Thomas, John. "Older Women." *Running Times,* March 1983.

Track and Field News, October 1983.

"2:27:33—and Waiting." *The New York Times,* October 23, 1979.

Tyson, Molly. "Leaders of the Pack." *Women's Sports,* January 1981.

PART II: A RUNNER'S BODY: WHAT WOMEN WANT TO KNOW

Amdur, Neil. "Accord on Olympic Drug Tests Reached." *The New York Times,* November 10, 1983.

———. "The Toll Conditioning Can Take on Athletes." *The New York Times,* March 6, 1983.

"Anabolic-Androgenic Steroids in Sports." *The Physician and Sports Medicine,* March 1978.

Anderson, Col. James L., Ph.D., et al., eds. *The Yearbook of Sports Medicine 1982.* Chicago: Year Book Medical Publishers, Inc., 1982.

Baker, Elizabeth R., M.D. "Menstrual Dysfunction and Hormonal Status in Athletic Women: A Review." *Fertility and Sterility,* vol. 36, no. 6, December 1981.

"Birth Control Pill Finishes Last." *The Runner,* December 1983.

Borms, J., et al., eds. *Women and Sport: An Historical, Biological, Physiological and Sportsmedical Approach,* vol. 14: Medical Sport. Basel, Switzerland: Karger, 1981.

Carlberg, Karen A., et al. "Body Composition of Oligo/Amenorrheic Athletes." *Medicine and Science in Sports and Exercise,* vol. 15, no. 3, 1983.

Combs, Margaret Ray. "By Food Possessed." *Women's Sports,* February 1982.

Dale, Edwin, M.D., et al. "Physical Fitness Profiles and Reproductive Physiology of the Female Distance Runner." *The Physician and Sports Medicine,* January 1979.

Diddle, Albert, M.D. "Athletic Activity and Menstruation." *Southern Medical Journal,* vol. 76, no. 5, May 1983.

"Factors Important to Women Participants in Vigorous Athletics." *Sports Medicine and Physiology,* W.B. Saunders Co., 1979.

Feicht Sanborn, Charlotte, M.S., et al. "Is Athletic Amenorrhea Specific to Runners?" *American Journal of Obstetrics and Gynecology,* vol. 13, no. 8, August 15, 1982.

Ferstle, Jim, ed. "Runner's Anemia." *Running Times,* January 1981.

Frisch, Rose E., Ph.D., et al. "Delayed Menarche and Amenorrhea of College Athletes in Relation to Age of Onset of Training." *Journal of the American Medical Association,* vol. 246, no. 14, October 2, 1981.

Harris, Dorothy, M.D. "Update: Women's Sports Medicine." *Women's Sports,* February 1979.

The Health Letter, vol. XVII, no. 6, March 27, 1981.

Henry, Sherrye, Jr. "The Price of Perfection." *The Runner,* March 1982.

Hunter, Letha Y., M.D., and Carol Torgan. "The Bra Controversy: Are Sports Bras a Necessity?" *The Physician and Sports Medicine,* vol. 10, no. 11, November 1982.

Jopke, Terry. "Pregnancy: A Time to Exercise Judgment." *The Physician and Sports Medicine,* vol. 22, no. 7, July 1983.

Macdougall, Duncan. "Anabolic Steroids." *The Physician and Sports Medicine,* vol. 11, no. 9, September 1983.

MacLeod, Sheila. *The Art of Starvation: A Story of Anorexia and Survival.* New York: Schocken Books, 1982.

Mahle Lutter, Judy, M.A., and Susan Cushman. "Menstrual Patterns in Female Runners." *The Physician and Sports Medicine,* vol. 10, no. 9, September 1982.

Oglesby, Carole A. *Women and Sport: From Myth to Reality.* Philadelphia: Lea & Febiger, 1978.

Parrish, Michael. "Exercising to the Bone." *Women's Sports,* April 1983.

"The Participation of the Female Athlete in Long-Distance Running." *Sports Medicine Bulletin,* vol. 15, no. 1, January 1980.

Plowman, Sharon A., and Patricia C. McSwegin. "The Effects of Iron Supplementation on Female Cross Country Runners." *Journal of Sports Medicine,* 1981.

"Pregnant Women Advised to Consider Exercise Risks" (Brief Reports). *The Physician and Sports Medicine*, vol. 10, no. 2, February 1982.

"Pseudoanemia and Distance Runners." *Nike Wear Testing Newsletter*, vol. 1, no. 2; Winter 1983.

Robb, Sharon. "Running Champ Battles Anorexia in the Biggest Race—for Her Life." *Fort Lauderdale News and Sun-Sentinel*, May 7, 1983.

Roy, Steven, M.D., and Richard Irvin, A.T.C., Ed.D. *Sports Medicine—Prevention, Evaluation, Management, and Rehabilitation*. Englewood Cliffs,

———. "Sports Gynecology." New Jersey: Prentice-Hall, Inc., 1983.

———. "Sports Gynecology." *Running New Jersey*, February 1982.

"7 Women Athletes Banned for Drugs." *The New York Times*, October 26, 1979.

Shangold, Mona M., M.D. "Evaluating Menstrual Irregularity in Athletes." *The Physician and Sports Medicine*, vol. 10, no. 2, February 1982.

———. "Coach of the Year." *Runner's World*, January 1983.

———. "Sports Gynecology." *Running New Jersey*, May 1983.

———. "Sports Gynecology." *Running New Jersey*, July 1983.

———. "Sports Gynecology." *Running New Jersey*, September 1983.

———. "The Woman Runner: Her Body, Her Mind, Her Spirit." *Runner's World*, July 1981.

———. "Women's Running." *Runner's World*, January 1982.

Stern, Susan. "Side Effects—Birth Control and Athletic Performance." *Women's Sports*, April 1983.

Ullyot, Joan L., M.D., *Running Free*. New York: Perigee Books, 1980.

Yates, Alayne, M.D., et al. "Running—An Analogue of Anorexia." *New England Journal of Medicine*, vol. 308, no. 5, February 3, 1983.

PART III: RUNNING AND WINNING

Averbuch, Gloria. "Hanna Sheziffi: Racin' in the Sun." *Women's Sports*, January 1976.

Friedan, Betty. "Twenty Years After the Feminine Mystique." *The New York Times Magazine*, February 27, 1983.

"A Giant Leap Forward for 8,000 Women." *The Evening Press* (Dublin, Ireland), June 13, 1983.

"Harassment on the Run." *Runner's World*, February 1983.

Holman, Mitten and Bonnie Parkhouse. "Trends in the Selection of Coaches for Female Athletes: A Demographic Inquiry." *Research Quarterly for Exercise and Sport*, vol. 52, no. 1.

"It Was Simply Fantastic!" *The Evening Press* (Dublin, Ireland), June 13, 1983.

Kauss, David R. *Peak Performance: Mental Game Plans for Maximizing Your Athletic Potential.* Englewood Cliffs, New Jersey: Prentice-Hall, Inc., 1980.

Kidd, Thomas R., and William F. Woodman. "Sex and Orientations Toward Winning in Sport." *Research Quarterly for Exercise and Sport,* vol. 46, December 1975.

Liquori, Marty, and John L. Parker. *Real Running.* Wideview Books, 1982.

"Marathon Month." *Track and Field News,* May 1983.

Roughton, Henley. "Not for Women Only." *Footnotes,* vol. 11, no. 3, Fall 1983.

PART IV: PREDICTIONS

Baster-Brooks, Christine. "The Number Crunchers." *New Zealand Runner,* November/December 1982.

"Battle of the Sexes." *Women's Sports,* June 1981.

Dyer, K.F., and Bob Wischnia. "Why Men Run Faster Than Women." *Runner's World,* November 1983.

Nelson, Bert. "People and Things." *Track and Field News,* November 1983.

Wood, P.S. "Sex Differences in Sports." *The New York Times Magazine,* May 18, 1980.

Index

About the Author

GLORIA AVERBUCH is a runner and a writer. She has directed public relations for the world's largest running organization, the New York Road Runners Club, since 1979. She announces major national and international races and has her own year-round radio program on WABC Radio in New York. She is married to national class marathoner Paul Friedman.